Thinking Outside the Ballot Box

Matthew Garr

Table of Contents

This book is dedicated to everyone who sees the world as it is, and recognizes it's not all it can be. Here's to the never-ending journey of improvement.

Foreword

If you're reading this book, I would like to thank you. Just by looking at its cover, flipping through the pages, or even skimming the Foreword, you're demonstrating at least some form of interest in the political process; and how we can make it better. As I write these words, there are two emotions that I believe best describe our current, collective political consciousness: confusion and fear. This book's objective is to alleviate at least the former, while I believe that a better understanding of the political process could provide a first step towards resolving the latter as well. The confusion, I think, doesn't stem from a lack of engagement or intelligence. I think that people, in general, have a very good grasp of how politics and policy affects their daily lives. We're not politically ignorant or stupid by any means. We're very aware of the effects that politics have on us, even if we're not always quite sure about how these policies came to be. How we put food on the table, where we work, and even where we live are all affected by political decisions at every level, from local city councils and school boards, to state legislatures, all the way to the halls of Congress and the Oval Office of the presidency. No, I think that we have a very good idea of how policy affects us. However, what is often just a little bit more difficult to piece together is how and why these policies are created, and what processes are at play when doing so. Often, the problem with piecing this policy-making process together is that we simply don't have the time in our days to become experts in political science just so that we can enact our own will on legislation that affects us. We're too busy doing other important things, so trying to better understand the political process can easily fall to the wayside. That time problem is what this book hopes to counteract. In a manageable amount of time, I hope this book can provide a springboard for the political exploration of all who read it and help you find answers to the questions: Where do I stand? What types of policies affect me and the people I care about? How can I use my knowledge of the political system to enact my will and beliefs upon it, to better my life and the lives of those around me? With knowledge comes power, and with power comes agency. Upon reading this book, my hope is that you, the reader, will be able to discover some sense of political agency—a belief that you do indeed have some power in this chaotic political world we live in. You might not even need to read the whole book, and that's okay. This book is meant to be a reference, a way to fill in those blind spots in your knowledge that we all have (I know I sure do).

Additionally, this book will likely challenge some of your beliefs and preconceived notions about how politics works. While the book is based in fact, everything we do is informed by our biases, opinions, and worldviews. Sometimes, your worldview will diverge from mine, and that's okay. In fact, I wouldn't want it any other way. Throughout the course of the book, you'll read some things you completely agree with, and some things that might be completely incongruent with your belief system. Take it as a challenge, if you will, and as an opportunity to look at the world from a slightly different perspective. Some of my favorite conversations have been with friends that I completely disagree with. While they are sometimes frustrating endeavors, these conversations are often much more positive and rewarding experiences than simply preaching to the choir. I don't expect you to believe everything that you see here, and I very much welcome my vision and beliefs being challenged. However, I do hope that you continue to read, even if it's just to counter what I'm saying. After all, this book isn't meant to be a polemic or a debate, but a journey to be undertaken together. If you're reading this, it's probably safe to say that you're either confused or concerned to some degree about the state of government. Hopefully, by the end of this book, we'll be able to move forward as allies, united in the goal of improving the structure and function of government, even if we're divided on exactly which path to take.

I truly believe that understanding the political system is a journey that can only be undertaken with a reliable guide, and I hope to show through sharing my background that I can be that reliable guide for you. My name is Matthew Garr, and I'm a young political writer from just outside of Kansas City writing his debut book. I'm not a politician. I'm not a city council member, a former mayor, or even a member of a school board. I'm not a lobbyist, a public figure, or a speechwriter. I'm simply someone devoted to thorough research who hopes to make politics just a bit more understandable for the people who are most affected by it. I firmly believe that a more educated public is one that can make the political process better for all involved. I also believe that the political process is currently broken, rigged in favor of higher powers who care little for the average citizen outside of receiving their votes or their dollars. My main goal with this book is to return democratic power and agency to the people who take vital part in the political process, amplifying their voices against the powers that be.

During the course of this book, I refer to the United States of America (the main government we will be considering) as a democracy, a system in which the individual citizens of a country have equal representation in its government. I do this not because I believe the country is currently a perfect democracy; indeed, we are far from it. We've come a long way from the one-person-one-vote system that was born in ancient Greece, and the current American system looks most favorably upon those with the most wealth. However, I believe that the ideals that democracy was founded upon still have a massive role to play in the course of the history and future of the United States. It's important to first note that for the vast majority of its history the United States has not been anywhere close to a true democracy. After all, the original Constitution only gave voting rights to white, male landowners. As time has passed, different groups have fought for and won the right to vote. However, even with universal suffrage, how much power do the people of the United States really hold, and how much of our politics is dictated by the money and power of different groups? Throughout the course of this book, I will give careful attention to how the United States has lived up to these democratic ideals, as well as the countless ways in which it has failed, and (most importantly) how we can fix it.

Many books have been written depicting the under-the-table inside deals of the halls of Congress, the unknown-to-the-public privileges of those in power, and the back stabbing and secret alliances between unlikely friends. This won't be that kind of book. I claim no insider information, and I believe that's for the best. We have a lot more power and agency than we think we do in enacting real change in our government, but much of our power comes from collective action and unity, something incredibly difficult to find. Finding and using this agency and collective power will be absolutely essential if we are to fix our democracy. The problems our democracy faces are myriad and imminent. The climate crisis threatens to burn us down and drown us. Income inequality is only growing in strength, as more and more are required to survive on less and less while the top few enjoy the spoils of a war they don't even know they're fighting. Extremists, both obvious and insidious, are threatening to take down our democracy through violence, political power, and the influence of egregious wealth. If we wish to address and solve these problems, it is imperative that the will of the people be reflected in their government. This journey will not be an easy one, but I truly believe that we will be able to find solutions, so long as we recognize that our ultimate enemy is the problems we face, not ourselves. While by no means do I expect perfect national unity—nor would I want anyone to give up their deeply held beliefs for the sake of it—it's essential to turn our focus away from each other's throats and towards the issues we collectively face. If I am successful, this book can hopefully provide a place to start.

Chapter 1: Collective Action

I'd like to begin with a thought experiment. Picture, for a moment, that you've been arrested for committing a crime. The crime itself doesn't really matter, nor does your innocence, but for simplicity's sake let's say that you robbed a shoe store with your friend Alexis and stole a pair of Jordans. Let's also pretend that your name is Jane. If your name is actually Jane, then your job is a bit easier. If your name is not Jane, then it's time to use the power of your imagination. The police take you into custody, separate you from Alexis, and say in no uncertain terms:

"Look. We know that you robbed the shoe store with your friend Alexis. We caught you in the act, Jordans in hand, and we want to put you away for a long time. However, we'll strike you a deal if you play a little game with us."

The game looks something like this:

1. **If both you, Jane, and your friend, Alexis, confess to robbing the shoe store, you'll both get three years in prison.**
2. **If Jane confesses, and Alexis doesn't, then Alexis gets off scot free, while Jane gets five years in prison. The converse (pun intended) occurs if Alexis confesses but Jane doesn't.**
3. **If neither Jane nor Alexis confess, then they both receive a four year sentence.**

Or, for those of you who like tables, the game looks something like this:

	Alexis doesn't confess	Alexis confesses
Jane doesn't confess	Both (4 years)	Jane (0), Alexis (5)
Jane confesses	Jane (5), Alexis (0)	Both (3 years)

So, as Jane, what do you do?

Based on real life experiments of the Prisoner's Dilemma,[1] the Jane character in this situation often chooses to keep quiet. However, why would Jane avoid confessing in this particular scenario?

In this scenario, Jane can either confess and receive more jail time on average (four years), or not confess and receive less jail time on average (two years) with a possibility of no jail time at all. Clearly, keeping quiet is the best option here.

However, what happens when we change the incentives?

Let's change the years of jail time just a bit, and our new decision table would look something like this:

	Alexis doesn't confess	**Alexis confesses**
Jane doesn't confess	Both (5 years)	Jane (0), Alexis (3)
Jane confesses	Jane (3), Alexis (0)	Both (2 years)

As Jane, would your decision change?

This particular iteration is a bit more difficult to determine. In both situations, Jane faces an average of 2.5 years of jail time. However, that average of 2.5 could look wildly different depending on her decision. Confessing to the crime guarantees Jane a stint in prison, but a relatively short one. On the other hand, staying silent gives Jane the chance of total freedom. . . or a much longer five-year prison sentence.. I truly don't envy Jane in making this decision, and at this moment other factors would begin to come into play. Does Jane have family on the outside, perhaps children? Would she have to start her career over if she spent any time in prison? Is she the bread winner of her family, and does she have others relying on her income? Some of these factors might lead her towards making the high risk, high reward choice of staying silent, hoping against hope that Alexis confesses.

Of course, this leads us to the other most important factor in the equation: Alexis. If Jane knows any of the answers to the previous questions about her friend Alexis, that can help her determine what he's going to do, and therefore what she should do. Of course, Alexis will be going through a similar thought process, but that's beside the point at the moment. If Jane knows that Alexis has already been to prison three times, she might be able to guess that he will confess and receive a certain, shorter prison time. If Jane knows that Alexis is a single parent of two, she might be able to ascertain that he will try to avoid prison time by choosing to stay silent.

So, you may be asking yourself, what does the Prisoner's Dilemma have to do with politics? Like most people, politicians have to make numerous decisions every day. However, the decisions that politicians make can have a huge impact on not only their constituents, but also on their chances of being re-elected. When a candidate decides to sign on to a piece of legislation (or unceremoniously shove it through a paper shredder), they're making a decision that they know will in some way impact their standing among their constituents. As can be expected, each constituent has their own policy priorities that drive their voting habits. In order for a politician to secure re-election, they need to either maintain the coalition of voters that brought them into office in the first place, or alter their emphasis on particular issues in order to match changing voter priorities. Often, there are two main ways that politicians can keep tabs on voters' positions and priorities: opinion polling and constituent services. From the perspective of the constituents, one of these is much more manipulable than the other. While opinion polling—which asks people where they stand on certain issues or candidates—can give politicians a good idea of where their constituents stand (provided the sample is representative), activists hoping to influence the behavior of politicians can't really do much to influence people to answer one way or another. In addition, opinion polling often isn't completely representative of if a particular position taken on an issue will actually cause a voter to cast their ballot for the politician or for their opponent. Often, it is merely an indicator of where voters stand on an issue or candidate at a particular point in time, and isn't necessarily predictive of how they will vote in the future. Constituent services, like helping someone fill out the necessary paperwork to receive their tax return, provide a better opportunity to predict voter behavior because they allow political operatives to see firsthand the issues that actually motivate their voters by interacting with them.

Have you ever called your representative, senator, or another politician to let them know your thoughts on a position they've taken? If so, you probably remember how it went. You dialed their number, called their office, and briefly spoke about (or yelled about) the issue to some poor intern whose entire job is to sit there and speak with (or get yelled at by) constituents. Don't worry too much, they probably knew what they were getting themselves into. After your hasty monologue, the intern asked you for your name and zip code, thanked you for your input, and told you that they will pass on the message. From there, you hang up, unsure about how much good was actually done from berating some poor intern who actually has nothing to do with the policy being passed. Hold that thought.

Jumping onto the other side of the phone, the intern likely hangs up, mentally dusts themselves off, and then pulls up a giant spreadsheet. Into this spreadsheet, they enter your name, zip code, and a coded version of the issue(s) you spoke to them about, as well as your position on the issue. After doing so, they brace themselves in preparation for the next call. Now, it's possible you're starting to recognize why constituent services are much more manipulable from a voter's perspective than opinion polling. In opinion polling, the sample is carefully determined by the polling company to be as accurate as possible. In constituent services, the sample is exactly what the constituents want it to be. As many or as few people can call the office as they want to, and if a politician's office receives a barrage of calls from angry citizens, they're much more likely to pay attention. In addition, in keeping record of constituent calls, politicians are able to pay close attention to the exact issues that *most* affect and appeal to their potential voters. This is where the Prisoner's Dilemma comes in.

Let's say, now, that our new friend Emily is the representative for Texas's 15th congressional district, one currently rated (as of July 2022) as an evenly divided toss-up by FiveThirtyEight, an organization that aggregates political polling in order to determine the most likely outcome.[2] Emily will face re-election this November, and wants to secure as many voters as possible before Election Day. In her district, one of the popular hot-button issues has been, say, the use of eminent domain to level a housing development to create a parking garage for the nearby City Hall. Emily, an advocate for protecting inner-city housing, has rallied against the parking garage, and it looks like the political pressure is starting to have some success. However, in the weeks before the wrecking crew arrives, hundreds of business owners in the community call into Emily's office. They ask her to come out in support of the new parking garage because it will allow for more customers to park in town and frequent their businesses. In quick succession, a polling firm surveys 1,000 locals of the area and finds that 55% of the population surveyed is in favor of keeping the housing intact. Will Emily potentially change her tune and support building the parking garage?

In this particular scenario, it's possible that Emily will change her mind. Even though over half of the population is in favor of keeping the housing, the people who feel the strongest about the parking garage would prefer to level the housing development. Briefly sidestepping the fact that these business owners (and undoubtedly lobbyists) have likely financially contributed to Emily's re-election campaign, their voices alone could have been enough to change Emily's mind, even against the majority of the population. Is it possible that Emily has guessed wrong and will lose her re-election campaign? Yes. However, this isn't how the story always needs to end. If the neighbors who live in the housing development, as well as other members of the sympathetic 55% put together a call-in or write-in campaign, their collective voices can outweigh those of the business owners. Even with financial contributions from the business owners, Emily might stand firm in her decision to save the housing development if she is convinced that bulldozing it would reduce her re-election prospects.

This scenario shows a possible truth of our political system. When they act together, and only when they act together, groups of individuals in pursuit of a common goal are able to impact how the political system functions. If they work together, citizens can change the incentives of the Prisoner's Dilemma, making certain consequences much more salient than others. This is where we begin to run into some difficulties because, of course, different people have different opinions. Even when voters agree on a general policy goal, it's possible that everyone has a slightly different preference for how to achieve that goal. Suppose, for example, that everyone in a political party agrees we need to cut taxes to reduce the size of government. Different party members may have different ideas for which programs or services to reduce funding for, or even cut out entirely. Some voters might believe that our military is overfunded, and we should cut back on military spending unless there's a credible threat. Other voters could support private education and want to reduce state and local taxes that fund public schools. Still other voters might believe in anarchist principles, and want to rid themselves of burdensome government entirely so that we can all live free of State intervention. Naturally, not everyone agrees on one idea, and we're just focusing on those individuals who want a smaller government. There's a whole other, similarly large faction who want a larger, more robust government, with a myriad of opinions about how much larger and how much more robust, and in what ways. With all this complexity, it's surprising that political parties or coalitions can get *anything* done.

Our aforementioned difficulties in determining government funding represent something called a Collective Action Problem, or a problem that occurs when individuals have a common goal, but don't entirely agree on the route to take in order to achieve said goal.[3] In order to actually achieve the goal in a timely manner, two important things must occur:

1. A common method of achieving the goal, or a road map, must be established.
2. A way to ensure that all members of the group are equally working towards said goal must be established.

Let's start with the road map and talk about group strength and cohesiveness after. If we hope to ensure that our road map actually leads to our intended destination, we need as many people to be on board with the map as possible. Keep in mind that for every group of people working towards an intended policy, there is often a similarly sized group working just as hard to make sure that policy doesn't pass. As such, if we want to successfully beat the other group, we need to be even more committed to our course of action than they are to theirs. Of course, this is difficult considering the differences of opinion represented across any group of people. So, what should be the first step in determining a plan that can balance the needs of as many people as possible? One method would be to figure out the one plan that most people can agree on. There's one key, tried, and true way of doing so: democracy.

There's more than one way to hold a Democratic election. In our case, one way that we might want to focus on looks similar to a ballot initiative. In ballot initiatives, a particular issue or policy is presented to voters, who then self-determine whether or not they agree with passing the policy measure. Ballot initiatives are often restricted to state or local elections, but for our example, let's pretend that the Small Government Party (not a real party as far as I know) is using one to determine what part of their collective platform should look like. In our case, the ballot initiative would look something like this:

SMALL GOVERNMENT PARTY INITIATIVE 2D: THE SMALL GOVERNMENT PARTY OF THE UNITED STATES OF AMERICA SHALL REDUCE THE SIZE AND SCOPE OF THE FEDERAL GOVERNMENT AND REDUCE ITS DEBT BY ADVOCATING FOR WHICH OF THE FOLLOWING:

- REDUCE FUNDING FOR THE MILITARY IN PEACETIMES BY 20%
- REDUCE FUNDING FOR THE DEPARTMENT OF EDUCATION BY 15%
- GRADUALLY DOWNSIZE THE BUDGET OF EACH DEPARTMENT BY 5% EACH YEAR

- IMMEDIATELY CEASE ALL SERVICES PROVIDED BY THE FEDERAL GOVERNMENT AND CLOSE ALL OFFICES THEREOF INDEFINITELY

Somewhat unrealistic examples, I know, but they work for our purposes. Ideally, the winning plan would provide party leaders with a better idea of which plan to pursue. The best plan is the one that most party members support. . . or at least the one that enough members support to actually win against the opposing party. Outside of democratic ballot initiatives—which in America usually only occur a couple of times state-wide each election cycle—another possible solution is one that American readers might find more familiar: the election of representatives.

In this case, an election would be held in which members of each faction of the party could run for party leadership and therefore have agenda-setting powers. Rather than having party members vote for the *plans* themselves, this form of democracy allows individuals to vote for fellow *members* who they believe will best represent their interests once in power. This form of democracy requires speeches, debates, and candidate forums to test the skills and ability of candidates to fight for their ideals. These features increase the likelihood that the individual eventually elected into the position of power will be a capable advocate for their plan. Candidate based elections are distinctly different to the ballot measure option which could potentially go against the will of those in power. This distinction is especially important when we consider the second key difficulty of solving collective action problems: ensuring that all parties involved are working equally hard to solve the problem.

I'm sure that you've worked as part of a group project before, be it at school, at work, or elsewhere. If not, I envy you. Take a moment to think back on the times you spent working as a group. Was most of the work equally divided? Did some members do more work than others? Did some members of your group not do any work at all? As you've probably experienced, that mythical equally-balanced group project is incredibly hard to find. You probably won't be surprised to find out that a similar dynamic exists in politics as well. In every group, there are factions seeking to accomplish as much as possible by working as little as possible, and others seeking to do anything they can to just get the job done. Of course, the stakes here are quite a bit higher, increasing the negative impacts of the slackers. Political battles take a lot of collective energy (significantly more than your ECON 101 group project, unfortunately) and working as a unit can be the difference between success and failure. Naturally, one of the priorities of any political leader is making sure that the people who support them are on board with their agenda. Or, at least more on board with their agenda than with another's. While they have a head start by having been selected as the most liked candidate, they need to recognize that not everyone will be as excited about their election as their most fervent supporters. As you can imagine, it's the stragglers and dissenters who are the most likely to socially loaf, or not give their all in pursuit of the policy goal. Some might actually actively work against it. In order to avoid any negative repercussions from these groups of people at the ballot box, political leaders might rely on their skills of argument and persuasion to fight to persuade those who might need just a bit more convincing. Here is where having a strong figurehead is important. If a policy goal is agreed upon and becomes part of the platform for a political party, the leaders of said party might not necessarily support said policy as much as the members who voted for it. This lack of cohesion makes it difficult for party leadership to discourage slacking off, as they might be doing it themselves. However, having the presence of a strong leader working for change is a powerful incentive for party members to similarly push for the change that a majority of the party hopes to see come to fruition.

Before we move on, let's jump back to our parking garage example. In the fight between preserving the neighborhood and building a parking garage, there are two main forces at play. First, the successful (or unsuccessful) collective action of each side will make Emily more likely to pick one side or another, in order to increase her chances of re-election. This represents one key feature of successful collective action: bringing authority figures to your side. Once Emily supports one side or the other, the second positive effect of collective action occurs. As a local representative in a position of power, Emily brings authority to her chosen side. Additionally, her presence rouses the support of her side, giving them a leader to rally around and boosting their chances of success.

At this point, you may find yourself asking: Where do *I* come into this? What role can *I* play? Even if you don't currently hold political office, which is true for the majority of people, you can still play a meaningful role in maximizing the effectiveness of collective action. Find an issue or policy that moves you. See what the local chapter of a political advocacy group, city council, or state government has to say about it. You can attend meetings, talk to friends and family, vote in local and national elections, or even run for office yourself. While leadership roles can certainly be frustrating, changes are made by the people in the group project who are actually taking charge and participating. By participating, and encouraging those around you to do the same, you might just feel like you're beginning to have an impact.

Chapter 2: Where our Government Began

This is the point in the book where everything I write becomes more America-centric. This is not due to any particular deference to the government of the United States, or a belief that it is necessarily superior to other forms of government. The Constitution of the United States is far from a perfect document, and it is one that is a work in progress. Rather, I believe that the government of the United States of America occupies a particularly interesting place in global politics, namely that it has the oldest codified constitution in the world. Technically, the oldest constitution (at a whopping 400 years old at the time of writing) belongs to San Marino, an independent enclave within the borders of Italy. However, not all of its original elements are currently the law of the land, so we will be focusing on the United States's constitution as an example of longevity.[4] The average constitution lasts about 17 years,[5] falling out of existence roughly one year before it would have given itself the right to vote, provided it was a sentient and upstanding citizen of its country. While length is far from the only indicator of a "good" constitution (after all, a constitution enforced at gunpoint might just last a long time), it's a decent indicator of its ability to maintain societal order, as well as stay relevant as times change. Also, a constitution's length allows us to survey how it has changed over time, a necessary element for its effectiveness. In order to understand why the United States's Constitution has lasted so long, it might be a good idea to take a look at what other features make national constitutions effective to begin with.

The word "constitution" can refer to multiple things. Apart from the general rules and guidelines that dictate the basic structure of a government (a Constitution with a capital C, we'll call it), a constitution (emphasis on lowercase c) can additionally refer to one's physical or mental state. A cancer patient can suffer from "a weakened constitution," as can someone dealing with depression or anxiety. In order to ensure that their constitution is strong, a person must actively work on it.

A person working to build a strong constitution might eat nutritious meals, stay active, take vitamins and supplements, attend annual doctor's appointments, practice self care, attend regular therapy, etc. If an individual keeps their body in tip-top shape, they'll likely live longer, healthier lives. Just as a person works to make their constitution strong, a country's citizens and government officials must take frequent, active steps to ensure that their Constitution is strong as well. The International Institute for Democracy and Electoral Assistance (IDEA) outlines numerous rules and fundamentals for what should, in theory, make a Constitution as strong as possible. While IDEA's guidelines are far from the only ones explaining what makes Constitutions adequate or inadequate, they represent an authoritative figure on democracy on the world's stage, and have helped member states around the world strengthen their democratic institutions. Using their outline, as well as a slightly corny human body analogy, we can take a look at why America's Constitution has endured, and why others fall out of existence after 17 years.

IDEA proposes that Constitutions must organize power horizontally and vertically, express a country's identity, limit and direct state powers, and recognize international law. Additionally, they claim that a Constitution must not become too entrenched in dictating specific laws—as nobody can accurately predict what the future will look like—or dictate how these laws will be enforced by the future individuals in power. Because of this, Constitutions need to be flexible and must provide mechanisms for future change or amendment.[6] Now, let's take a look at each of these concepts individually so we can understand how to create a Constitution that can protect the rights of all and evolve with changing times.

I. Constitutions must disperse powers horizontally

First and foremost, it's important to define what we mean by horizontal power. This kind of power is distributed across the same level of government. Horizontal distribution can be on the local, state, or national level (as states themselves often have their own Constitutions), but must stay on that level. Otherwise we're talking about vertical power, which I'll explain in a moment. Using the United States as an example, the Constitution divides power horizontally by establishing three different branches of government: Executive, Legislative, and Judicial.[7] If you're an American and remember from your Civics classes (and if not, that's absolutely okay, that's why we're here), each branch of government specializes in a particular area of governance. We'll take a closer look at the role of each branch in later chapters, but I think just having a basic understanding is sufficient at this point. The Legislative branch is divided into two subsections: the House of Representatives and the Senate. Charged with the creation of laws, this branch must pass and reconcile bills through both sections in order to send said bills to the President's desk to be signed into law. The Executive branch, headed by the President, is tasked with the enforcement of laws. To do so, the President relies on a cabinet of administrative officials divided into different bureaucratic departments. The Judicial branch, the third and final branch of the United States's government, uses the country's Constitution to determine the legality and veracity of its laws. The Supreme Court, the highest court within the Judicial branch, has the final say on Constitutional disputes and can attempt to provide clarity when the Constitution doesn't seem to indicate the legality or illegality of a particular action.

Let's return to our Constitution-constitution analogy. It seems reasonable to believe that horizontal power is akin to one's mental constitution, as shown by the brain. The brain itself displays similar divisions of power, as physically distinct areas are associated with the functions of our thought, emotion, language, personality, behavior, and our five senses and how we perceive them. Additionally, the different areas of our brain must be able to work together simultaneously, without the dominance of one region over another. Can you imagine if every time you heard a noise, you went momentarily blind? Or if every time you thought something to yourself, you lost your sense of smell? Our brains require the simultaneous function of multiple different regions, and if one dominates over the others, it spells real trouble for us.

Often, what occurs during mental illness is similar to the domination of one part of your brain over another. In those who experience anxiety, activation of the fight or flight response can cause your brain to signal for the release of hormones that prevent them from relaxing, and can even cause their immune system to malfunction. Depression works similarly, often keeping one from experiencing life with the same color and energy as before. On the flip side, addiction can occur when a different part of the brain is in control, as chasing the highs of the addiction begins to take over your life. In these cases, too much of a good thing becomes a bad thing. Naturally, in order for our brains to work properly, we need to ensure that one part of the brain can't dominate the others, at least not outside of our control. Likewise, creators of the Constitution created institutional rules ensuring that one part of government can't dominate the others. The system that sprang from this is called checks and balances, and it ensures that for every power one branch of government has, one of the other branches of government has a similar power that keeps it in check. Some of the examples of checks and balances in the American Constitution are as follows:

- **The Executive branch can enforce laws, but the Legislative branch can impeach the president and the Judicial branch can declare their enforcement procedures unconstitutional**
- **The Legislative branch can create laws, but the Executive branch can veto said laws and the Judicial branch can declare laws unconstitutional**
- **The Judicial branch can interpret the constitutionality of laws, but the Executive branch appoints justices to the courts and the Legislative branch approves federal judges**

Just like a brain can only function when its different regions are working in tandem, a government can only function if one branch doesn't have unchecked power over the others. If a Constitution hopes to adequately divide powers horizontally, it must ensure that one division can't go rogue and control the others if some power-hungry politician or judge decides they want more power than they already have.

Horizontal distribution of power is where the United States has begun to run into trouble. As will be explained more in the chapters regarding each branch of government, the Executive and Judicial branches in particular seem to have outgrown the system of checks and balances, at least when compared to previous governments of the United States. The amount of Executive Orders issued by each president since FDR has dwarfed previous presidents, meaning that presidents are choosing to more unilaterally dictate policy enforcement throughout the duration of their terms. Additionally, Federal and Supreme Court justices have become more likely to show their true partisan colors, and scandals like Clarence Thomas's failure to disclose hundreds of thousands of dollars worth of luxury gifts and trips from Republican mega donor Harlan Crow have shown that Supreme Court justices must be held to a higher standard, or risk losing the faith of the American people.[8] A horizontal division of power only works when power is equally distributed, and it appears that the United States is beginning to fall short.

Next, we'll explore how Constitutions require a vertical distribution of power as well.

II. Constitutions must disperse powers vertically

As horizontal power refers to how power is dispersed across the same level of government, vertical power is dispersed across different levels of government. One of the most common methods of dispersal is through gradually scaling down the powers of government from the national to the local level. In the United States, the Constitution divides power among three separate levels: National, State, and Local. Altogether, this system of division is historically referred to as Federalism.[6] However, in the drafting of the Constitution (and for decades afterwards), there was much debate as to what exactly this Federalism should look like. While we'll leave some of the details of this debate to the later chapter on political parties, one of the United States's first divisions (aside from the whole revolution thing) was between the aptly named Federalists and Anti-Federalists. The Federalists, led by Alexander Hamilton, James Madison, and John Jay, sought a Constitution that concentrated power in a strong central government. The National level of government would have the most control, while state and local governments would be able to manage the smaller issues that the National government didn't have time to manage, such as the building and upkeep of roads and bridges. The Anti-Federalists, as political parties go, were slightly less well structured. They shared a common disregard for the Constitution, due to the increased power of the Federal Government it espoused, but they weren't able to agree on one particular government to counter the Federalist's plan.

If you remember from the first chapter what happens to political factions that can't agree on one roadmap, you'll probably understand what happened to the Anti-Federalists, and why they were unable to stop the Constitution from being ratified. However, they didn't leave empty handed, as Anti-Federalist pressures led to Madison's creation of a Bill of Rights, giving rights to American citizens that couldn't be infringed upon by the Federal Government.[10] The lack of Anti-Federalist power didn't persist, and after Federalist or Federalist-friendly presidents such as George Washington and John Adams, the Anti-Federalists were able to successfully unify around a criticism of the size and scope of government under the banner of the rebranded Democratic Republicans.

As you can see, the debate over the vertical dispersal of powers was one of the leading problems facing our founding fathers, and for good reason. As America had recently won a war against an overbearing central government in Great Britain, and the Articles of Confederation written immediately after the victory had proved too small of a Federal Government, America's founders must've felt like chemists tinkering with what came to be known as The Great Experiment, adding a little democracy to the concoction here, a little bit of state's rights there, and hoping that it wouldn't all explode in their faces. Continuing our constitution-Constitution analogy, the right combination of local, state, and national power for a healthy government is something similar to consuming all of the nutrients necessary for a healthy life. While the exact proportions of a balanced diet have been debated (and several books could be written about the role agricultural lobbyists played in the creation of these guidelines), general consensus indicates the "best" diet consists of balancing carbohydrates, vegetables, fruits, protein, and dairy, in descending order of importance. I'm sure you've all seen the food pyramid, or the food portion plate, often displayed proudly above elementary cafeteria lunchrooms that, oddly, rarely actually succeed in instilling these values among its students. Maybe that was just me. Anyway, adequately creating a vertical balance between layers of government can be seen as analogous to creating a properly balanced meal. Load your plate up with too much of a Federal Government, and you'll be spread too thinly to adequately address the small-scale problems that citizens face at the local level. I don't think anyone expects Congress to try to pass laws to fix potholes in Lindsborg, Kansas. However, if you add too much of Local or State government, you run into the problem of having incredibly diverse laws in neighboring cities. I mean, could you imagine traveling from St. Louis, Missouri to East St. Louis, Illinois and immediately having to change lanes and drive on the left side of the road? Sure, we could assume competency and hope that neighboring cities would keep driving on the same side of the road, but with a goverment too decentralized, few guard rails (road pun intended) would be in place to keep something like that from occurring.

In the United States, two concepts have been used to attempt to solve the power dispersal problem: Dillon's rule and Home rule. At the federal level, Congress can set certain laws for all Americans, but these laws can be overturned or upheld at the state level (think of how the age requirement for driver's licenses differs from state to state). However, at the level of the state and local legislature, things become a little bit more murky. According to Dillon's rule, local municipalities only have the powers explicitly delegated to them by their state governments. That is, a city or town can only perform actions and exercise power that their state gives to them in its Constitution. But, Home rule states that cities, towns, and local governments can perform actions and exercise any power that is not explicitly denied to them by the State. In this case, these municipalities are able to exercise relatively free reign, at least until the State government steps in and tells them otherwise by passing a law against it.[11] Across the United States, the majority of states use Dillon's rule, while a minority accept some variation of Home rule. This flexibility allows local governments to be as large or as small as its citizens need it to be, provided that its power doesn't infringe on that belonging to state or federal governments, of course.

III.   Constitutions must express a country's identity

We, the people, are divided. That much is incredibly evident. We're divided on the basis of politics, beliefs, religion, culture, race, sex, creed, ability, family, and much, much more. However, each and every one of us (hopefully) lives in a country that doesn't experience some form of civil war every time there's a national disagreement. Despite our differences in these categories, how are we able to stay (relatively) united? Odds are, no matter what country you live in, there's some form of national identity that supersedes many of its divisions, at least in everyday life. While many of these forms of national identity are only tangentially related to government, like national sports teams, federal holidays, or rituals such as national anthems, some forms of national identity are actually enshrined in a country's Constitution. One example of this in the United States's Constitution is its Preamble:

"We the People of the United States, in Order to form a more perfect Union, establish Justice, insure domestic Tranquility, provide for the common defense, promote the general Welfare, and secure the Blessings of Liberty to ourselves and our Posterity, do ordain and establish this Constitution for the United States of America."[7]

Notice exactly what type of wording goes into the Preamble. Union. Justice. Tranquility. Welfare. Secure the Blessings of Liberty to ourselves and our Posterity. What kind of red-blooded American could ever possibly disagree with that? In a way, that's the main point of this particular Preamble to the Constitution. It's kept purposely vague in order to appeal to a majority of individuals, even though these words mean different things to different people. Now, keep in mind what happens after these words. Does the Constitution indeed live up to its values, listed so preeminently at its beginning? After this Preamble was written, it took 75 years to stop enslaving African

Americans, and 20 more to extend to them the right to vote. It took a further 150 years for these words to apply to women, when they in turn secured the right to vote. It's important to note that even if a Constitution provides an excellent framework for equal rights and securing that elusive liberty and justice for all, it doesn't necessarily ensure that these rights will be put into practice. Rather, what a Constitution often does much better is outline what these rights *should* be, and provide a possible roadmap and the tools necessary in order to get there. What the U.S. Constitution often fails to do, in this particular case, is actually advance the policy to do so. I think that you'd be hard-pressed to find an American who doesn't hope for Justice, Tranquility, Welfare, and Liberty for as many people as possible. However, the way the Constitution was written, the United States didn't reach full suffrage until relatively recently, and has a ways to go before fulfilling the mandate outlined in the Preamble. Because of this, it's important that not only the Constitution, but also the identity expressed by the Constitution, should be responsive to the will of the people. If a particular mandate or identity no longer adequately represents the people, then it should be able to be changed through the same democratic processes that mold and shape the rest of the government.

In this way, a Constitution can be compared to one's psychological sense of self, particularly the self that one hopes to be. We all have an ideal sense of self, a person or type of person that we aspire be. Perhaps you want to read more, or eat healthier, or spend more time with friends, or even get enough sleep at night. Personally, I want to write more things that can help people understand politics. If you're reading these words, I'm one step closer to achieving my ideal self. As we grow closer and closer to our ideal self, we become more confident and mentally healthy as we recognize that we're on the right path. On the other hand, if we perform actions or say things that contrast with our ideal self, that's when we're likely to struggle with our mental—or even physical—health. A Constitution declares: "This is what we want to ideally be as a country. This is who we want to be, and this is how we get there." Unfortunately, this perfect ideal is not always reached. In fact, it is rarely ever reached, and sometimes an ideal that seems immutable at first can even change drastically over time, as the hopes and priorities of citizens change over time. It's particularly important to notice here that as these hopes and priorities shift, the Constitution needs to be able to change to suit them. The original Constitution was written by dozens of white, male landowners. In absolutely no world could the Constitution they came up with have fit the needs of even a majority of Americans then, let alone 200 years later. And yet, the vast majority of the Constitution remains the same, with just 27 amendments in almost 250 years, and none at all in the past 30 years. In order to truly reflect a country's identity, a Constitution must be flexible enough to actually be changed when necessary.

IV. Constitutions must be flexible

There's an important, relatively novel concept in educational psychology research that contrasts two different ways of looking at the world: Growth Mindset and Fixed Mindset. With credit to psychologist Carol Dweck, this contrast helps us to understand why some people succeed against adversity, while others flounder and fail when put to the test. To put it simply, individuals with a Growth Mindset tend to recognize that they're not necessarily the best versions of themselves, and that this isn't a bad thing. Rather, people with Growth Mindset recognize that with work and time, they can improve themselves in any discipline they want to. Even if they're not good at something right now, they recognize that they can work hard to make it a strength in the future. One strength that people with a Growth Mindset often exhibit is the ability to learn from their failures; and from constructive criticism. When someone with a Growth Mindset fails, they don't consider themselves a failure. They don't give up, or think that they're now bad at whatever skill they were practicing. Instead, the person picks themselves up, dusts themselves off, and considers what they can do next time to avoid failing in the future. A rather prominent example of this is Abraham Lincoln's road to the presidency. Lincoln lost elections for state representative, Speaker of the Illinois House of Representatives, Commissioner of the General Land Office, and the U.S. Senate before finally becoming President and ascending to the Oval Office after a long string of electoral failures.[12] It was important that, after each loss, Lincoln didn't think himself to be a bad legislator or politician, only that he needed to work harder in order to prove his political skill to voters.

A person with a Fixed Mindset, on the other hand, sees the world of talent in black and white. Someone with a Fixed Mindset can believe themselves to be good or bad at different things, but they believe that these talents are fixed in place. These individuals often gravitate towards what they're good at, and avoid what they're not. Because of this belief, their skills often won't change. They might continue to get better at what they're already good at, but they might be hesitant to take risks by working on their weaknesses due to the fear of failure. Additionally, failure can have a detrimental impact. If these individuals fail once, they're likely to believe that they'll fail again, often leading to a self-fulfilling prophecy.

So, you may be asking, what on earth could a Growth Mindset have to do with Constitutions? Well, this leads us to the fourth key feature of Constitutions: their flexibility. When a group of individuals, even incredibly well-informed and well-intentioned ones, write a Constitution, they must first and foremost realize that they will eventually be proved wrong about something. No matter how much foresight and preparation went into the agonizing hours of debate and discussion that occur when forming a government meant to last a millenia, its authors can only see so far into the future, and they can't expect this limited document to hold up indefinitely across time and space. Ideally, the writers must have a Growth Mindset. No matter how good this document is, there will come a day when some of its tenets will become outdated, unnecessary, or even may be found to be antithetical to its purpose. Heck, parts of this book you're reading will be deemed so at some point. That's why it's important for the authors of any Constitution to include mechanisms that allow it to change over time. Still, exactly *how* flexible constitutions need to be is another question altogether. How much flexibility is absolutely necessary, and how much will simply cause the document to snap under duress? The framers of the U.S. Constitution purposefully made it incredibly difficult to ratify changes. In order for Constitutional amendments to be passed, two-thirds of Congress or two-thirds of state legislatures need to agree for any amendment to simply be proposed. At that point, three-fourths of state legislatures or state conventions need to ratify the amendment in order for it to be made the law of the land. Honestly, it's a wonder how the U.S. Constitution has been amended a total of 33 times so far. The founders wanted to ensure that the Constitution couldn't be amended by some lone political group that managed to secure power, and it appears that they have succeeded in that venture at the very least. However, critics would posit that necessary societal reform can be held up by only one-fourth of states. The United States hasn't experienced a constitutional amendment since 1992, and indeed there have been 1,264 proposed (and failed) amendments to the Constitution coming from the Senate alone since the last one passed.[13]

One thing that the framers might not have been able to fully understand was the sheer power of division and political polarization that the United States would face years later. While the beginning of the United States certainly had its factions, it was coming off of a period of time where the country was united against a common enemy: Great Britain. After just winning the war for independence, fraternity was likely at a high during the time of the Constitutional Convention. It's possible that the framers could have overlooked the development of partisan polarization, and therefore believed that the high bar they set was reachable. Instead, as political polarization has rapidly increased in recent years,[14] America faces a much more divided environment than the founders did when they set precedents for amending the Constitution.

It's very possible that our currently divided state, combined with the high bar set by the Constitution's framers, will prevent any constitutional amendments from being considered for decades. If we hope to attempt to amend the Constitution any time soon, it appears that there are two major options: facilitate the amendment process, or take some major steps towards reducing the divisions between our political parties, and soon. Facilitating the amendment process would, unfortunately, require a constitutional amendment in and of itself. If the process was reformed by, for example, requiring only a three-fifths majority of Congress and State Legislators (or requiring only one or the other to achieve the majority), then certain constitutional amendments could be more in reach, while still maintaining a threshold that requires a sizeable majority.

Additionally, the process itself could be reformed. Some states hold semi-regular referendums on their constitutions, during which voters are asked if their state's constitution should be reformed. If a majority believes so, delegates gather together for a state constitutional convention, and propose changes. If the changes are accepted by voters, they're ratified in the state's constitution. A similar process at the state level, returning the power directly to voters rather than their representatives in power, would be a good way to put Constitutional ratification back in the hands of the people that it will most affect. If we were to require that each state hold a regular referendum on its state constitutions, with voters themselves deciding which parts need reformation, it could go a long way towards ensuring that the constitutions that guide state law are responsive to the will of the people it governs.

Of course, changes to the US constitution have been relatively rare, particularly in recent years. While some of this rarity stems from the high bar that needs to be cleared for amendments to be passed, the ever-increasing divisions between the left and the right, particularly within the halls of congress, has made this level of consensus even more difficult to find. While returning power back to the people would be a great place to start, it does us little good if the people themselves are hopelessly divided. In the next section, we'll consider political parties, one of the main vehicles of polarization in the United States.

Chapter 3: Political Parties

"However [political parties] may now and then answer popular ends, they are likely in the course of time and things, to become potent engines, by which cunning, ambitious, and unprincipled men will be enabled to subvert the power of the people and to usurp for themselves the reins of government, destroying afterwards the very engines which have lifted them to unjust dominion."

- George Washington's Farewell Address[13]

The first president of the United States made his stance on political parties crystal clear.[14] Two months later, partisan Federalist John Adams was elected to the presidency over Thomas Jefferson, a similarly partisan Democratic Republican. Oops. It's safe to say that we haven't heeded Washington's words ever since, even though it seems like many Americans still agree with him 250 years later. In fact, only about 19% of Americans claim that their preferred party actually lines up with most of their political views. This is especially odd, considering that the majority of Americans do indeed identify with some political party, even if they think that their views could be better represented by some other organization. Political parties are often decried as one of the most divisive mechanisms in government, and yet they have been an important fixture in America's political system since the country's founding. How can both of these facts be true? Do most Americans simply see political parties as a necessary evil, or is there some roadmap to a party-free country? To begin to answer this question, let's take a quick detour backwards towards the first chapter on Collective Action. In that chapter, you may remember that I outlined a problem to solve: Should the government be bigger or smaller, and how big or small should the government be? A very weighty question, and one that has indeed plagued America since the Federalist/Anti-Federalist debates at its conception. You may remember that we divided our electorate into several different groups, or factions, who all wanted some form of a smaller government, but disagreed on exactly what form. In the "reduce government" group alone, we had a variety of individuals who wanted to accomplish one of the following:

> **-Reduce funding for the military by 20%**
> **-Reduce funding for the Department of Education by 15%**
> **-Gradually downsize the budget of each department by 5% each year**
> **-Immediately cease all services provided by the Federal Government and close all offices immediately**

Seems like a pretty wide range of ideas, right?

Now, let's expand our debate just a little bit. Rather than only considering the individuals who want to reduce the size of the government, let's also bring in those who want to increase it. For our purposes, let's also create four separate factions that want to accomplish one of the following:

> **-Increase military funding by 20%**
> **-Increase funding for the department of education by 15%**
> **-Increase government spending to fund a variety of social services and public works projects**

-Increase government control over private businesses until the government provides every essential service

Now, the differences in public opinion seem a bit more myriad. So, what should each of the individual factions do? Let's say that there's an election approaching, and each one of the eight factions wants to elect a representative who is partial to their particular interests. In doing so, they want to make sure that the candidate they elect can accomplish two goals:

1: Run a platform that is as close to their ideal goals as possible
2: Have as good of a chance of winning as possible

Here is where some factions might run into a problem. Let's say, for instance, that each faction in the "reduce government" group runs their own candidate, with four candidates running in total. Everyone has a chance of their ideal platform winning, so everyone's happy. Next, the "increase government" group realizes that they can change the game to increase their chances of winning. Rather than running four individual candidates, they alter their strategy and decide to only run one. They determine (possibly by a vote) that among the four factions, the "Increase government spending to fund social services" faction has the most support, so they decide to only have that candidate run. When the general election occurs, the election results look something like this:

50%-Increase government spending to fund social services
14%-Reduce funding for the military by 20%
13%-Reduce funding for the Department of Education by 15%
12%-Gradually downsize the budget of each department by 5% each year
11%-Immediately cease all services provided by the federal government and close all offices immediately

The numbers might not play out as well in a real life example, but the group of voters with one candidate will often win easily. If the number of voters in each faction is relatively equal, then most voters in the group will recognize that even if a candidate doesn't exactly match their views, the one candidate that most matches their views is much better than any of the other party's alternatives. While three out of the four factions weren't perfectly represented by the social services candidate, they recognized that increasing the size of government was closer to their views than any of the other candidates who wanted to reduce the size of government, and so they voted accordingly. As you can see, this is one of the major pros of having political parties. Rather than attempting to work with incredibly loose and small coalitions of voters, parties allow voters to work together to ensure they elect a candidate that somewhat represents their values, even if they're not perfect. Overall, voters are looking for someone that takes them in the right direction, even if the candidate isn't exactly the final destination they're hoping for, and parties help voters to increase this probability.

Now, this improved ability to reach a consensus doesn't mean that political parties are anywhere close to being *only* good for the country. Perhaps, after all, there's another solution to the voting coalition problem listed above. What if, instead of allowing factions to coalesce into larger parties to win elections, we allowed only candidates from each faction alone? What if we had an election where a candidate ran espousing each viewpoint, instead of four from one party and one from the other? If that happened, the voting bloc might look a little bit more even, but with one key problem. If each of the factions were roughly equal, then each candidate would receive a roughly equal share of the vote, in this case about 12.5% of it. Now, who on earth wants to be the candidate who was only elected with 13% of the vote? What kind of mandate is that? Surely, the vast majority of voters (approximately 87% of them) would also be somewhat disappointed that the candidate they voted for didn't succeed, even if the successful candidate is somewhat similar in their policy goals. One thing that parties can do well is attempt to solve this problem by picking a consensus candidate that the majority of the party can agree on, leading to larger vote percentages for the winning candidate. However, this often stifles or completely silences opinions that don't necessarily fit into either of the major parties. Luckily, there's a solution that can not only ensure that majority opinions are represented, but also give a voice to those who might not necessarily fall into lockstep with a major party.

I'll further elaborate in the upcoming chapter on elections, but the vast majority of American states use what's called Open or Closed primaries to determine a party's standard bearer (Open and Closed simply refers to if the party allows or doesn't allow non-party members to vote in these elections). In both instances, all political parties hold primaries to vote for one candidate who will then represent them in the next round, or general election. In the general election, it's incredibly likely that either a Democrat or Republican will attain victory, as their groups of voters are simply larger than the other options, such as the Libertarian and Green parties. This leads to the Democrat vs. Republican binary that is a seemingly constant feature of America's government. However, for those of you who would prefer more minor party voices to enter the fray, there's another way of doing things. Currently, four different states[17] use what's called a top-two primary system, in which every single candidate running for office is entered into the same primary. At the end, the top two vote-getters advance to the general election, where the winner is selected. Now, instead of a minor party candidate needing to run against two major party candidates, a minor party candidate can run against a handful, a dozen, even tens of major party candidates in some cases. If you remember from our discussion above, this dilution of power among major parties makes it much more likely for a minor party candidate to sneak through and make it to the final round, where they only need to face off against one other candidate. For those of you who believe that more healthy political parties makes your country a more functioning democracy, advocating for top-two primaries could be a good place to start.

Americans reading this book might believe that being entrenched in a two-party system is a uniquely American problem. Fair enough, lots of American problems are uniquely American problems. However, due to the difficulties of truly achieving collective action, it's almost natural to find two dominating political parties in a democracy. Indeed, the United Kingdom is dominated by Labour and the Conservatives, Canada by the Liberals and Conservatives, and Spain by the Socialists and People's Party. What differentiates the United States from these other governments is easily seen by looking at the makeup of their legislative branches. In the United States, as of July 2022, the House of Representatives is made up of a total of 220 Democrats and 211 Republicans. The Senate, additionally, is split between 48 Democrats (and two progressive-leaning Independents) and 50 Republicans. If we look at the United Kingdom, however, Parliament is made up of 358 Conservatives, 200 from Labour, 44 Scottish National Party, 14 Liberal Democrat, nine Independents, eight Democratic Unionists, seven Sinn Fein, three Plaid Cymru (Welsh independence), two from both the Alba Party and Social Democratic and Labor Party, and one each from the Alliance and Green parties.[18] Without going into the details, I hope you take my word that the Spanish, French, Canadian, and many other legislative governments look similar to the UK's Parliament, and that the United States is actually relatively distinguished globally for its stricter adherence to a two-party system. While two parties certainly dominate the political landscape in these countries, they don't have a disproportionate voice in the government. While I'll delve further into how election systems differ across countries in the next chapter on elections, much of this minor party success stems from the election systems that these countries use. Often, instead of a primary system, these countries use either a first-past-the-post or a proportional representation system. First-past-the-post looks rather similar to the aforementioned top-two system, and has similar benefits, except the top vote-getter wins without needing to advance to a general election. This gives minor parties a further advantage, particularly if more major party candidates run. A proportional representation system, on the other hand, looks a bit different. In proportional representation, a country-wide general election is held in which citizens vote for parties, rather than candidates. A sample American version of the ballot would look something like this:

    ☐ Democratic Party
    ☐ Republican Party
    ☐ Libertarian Party
    ☐ Green Party
    ☐ Constitution Party
    ☐ Democratic Socialist Party

Depending on the election results, proportional numbers of seats in the Legislative branch would be allocated to each party. From that point, candidates are nominated and selected for each seat by either party officials or party members.

If we were to take America's 2020 presidential election results and transfer it to a proportional representation system, each chamber of our Legislative branch would look something like this, according to popular vote totals:[19]

House of Representatives
    Democratic Party- 223 Seats
    Republican Party- 204 Seats
    Libertarian Party- 5 Seats
    Green Party- 2 Seats

Senate
    Democratic Party- 51 Seats
    Republican Party- 47 Seats
    Libertarian Party- 2 Seats

As you can see, the results aren't much better than the party duopoly that controls America currently, but it does indeed give the Libertarian and Green party voices in the national legislative conversation that they would not have otherwise. Additionally, due to the contentiousness of the 2020 elections, most voters were persuaded to avoid voting for third party candidates in fear of letting the other party gain power. If people were incentivized to simply vote for their favorite candidate, without the fear of letting the other party win if they don't choose a more viable option, who knows how this representation could change?

There's one key detriment to a system with multiple strong parties, but it's actually one that has a pretty similar analogue in the U.S. Government. As those of you living in one of these parliamentary systems are likely aware, there's a rather difficult problem that's often referred to as "forming a government." In the United States, division of power is a relatively common occurrence. Sometimes Democrats have power, sometimes Republicans have power, but most of the time power is divided across each branch of government. This tends to work well enough, until a divided government can't agree on a federal budget, and the government temporarily shuts down. Oops. In systems with multiple major parties, this problem can sometimes be magnified. As more minority parties exist in the Legislative branch, it's much harder for one party to attain a majority strong enough to keep the government running by itself. Due to this difficulty, the party in power is often required to form allyships and coalitions with other parties, who decide to vote in the best interest of the party in power in exchange for being able to share in that power to some degree. This works relatively well, until one or more of the minority parties begins to feel like their needs aren't being met by the coalition, and they could subsequently back out of the power-sharing agreement. As it's hard to run a government when no majority can be reached to pass legislation, this can often be a pretty large problem. Unfortunately, one of the most common solutions to this problem is a rather costly and risky one: hold another election.

In parliaments that are determined by proportional representation, holding another election can be a powerful tool to shake up the political structures in place, form new allies, and try to form a majority again. However, running and ensuring the security of elections can be a costly endeavor, both in terms of monetary cost and cost to the reputation of the party that couldn't manage to form a majority. Holding another election runs the risk of ceding power to the other large party, particularly if their voters smell blood in the water. Sometimes, this constant shifting of powers can lead to decreased polarization, as each major party has to work with different minor parties each time, depending on voting results. Or, some countries end up holding a ridiculous amount of elections one after the other, as was the case in Israel, who had to hold five elections in four years from 2018-2022 as coalitions formed and fractured.[20] This can lead to voter apathy—not exactly a sign of a healthy democracy.

I would be remiss at this point in the conversation if I didn't point out another possible solution. If two parties can lead to division, and multiple parties can make consensus difficult to achieve, what other options do we have? Some countries have favored a one-party system in order to reduce divisions and try to streamline the electoral process. However, one-party systems really only tend to happen when one of two conditions are met:

1: Voters are similar enough to be adequately represented by the one-party platform
2: The one-party system is forced upon voters by an oppressive regime intending to quash dissent

The majority of one-party states that have existed or currently exist fall under one or more of the categories of Revolutionary, Marxist, or Fascist. In Africa, some of the more successful one-party states fall under the category of Revolutionary. In these cases, post-colonial governments were formed in which the only party that existed was an anti-colonialism party, fighting for the liberation of colonized forces in and around the country. But, as time passed, these countries tended to either split into a multi-party democracy, or become more authoritarian and turn into one-party dictatorships.[20] Other one-party states of this time period included Lenin's consolidation of Russia into the Communist party, as well as Hitler's establishment of the fascist Nazi party in Germany and Mussolini's attempts to do the same in Italy. Historically, it appears that one-party states are able to function well as unifying entities in the face of some significant threat, such as colonialism. However, over time, an unchallenged one-party state often succumbs to the temptations of authoritarianism, fascism, and dictatorship, upending the lives of ordinary citizens in the process. Currently, no one-party governments exist that are considered fully democratic, and aside from the beginning of political revolutions, one-party states seem to exist in counter to democratic principles, moreso the longer they remain in power.

So, where does this leave us? If one seeks to uphold democratic values, one-party systems appear to be best thrown out the window. Two-party systems often allow for more say in the primary process, but only for those in one of the two major parties. Multi-party systems can give a stronger voice to minor parties, and might even reduce division through coalition building, but often require heavy voter participation in the democratic process, as well as frequent inability to maintain said coalitions over long periods of time. Maybe your country offers the party system that works best for you, and maybe it doesn't. That's where you come in. Active political participation, collective action, and pressure of public officials are some of the best possible ways to ensure that your unique voice, and the voices of people like you, are heard as loudly and clearly as possible by those in power. In the next chapter, we'll take a closer look at the specifics of the election process, as well as how certain practices and processes can amplify or muffle the voice of the electorate. Political parties and the election process go hand in hand, as parties can often play a large role in how elections are administered, and therefore have a hand in the results of the elections themselves. If I accomplish my goal, the next chapter should allow us to recognize how political processes affect the results of elections, and the agency that we have as citizens to ensure that our own voices, rather than those of powerful interest groups, are heard.

Chapter 4: Elections and their Consequences

Elections are a cornerstone upon which democracy is built. In order for a democracy to stand, it must run free, fair, and honest elections. However, as the nature of the democratic system of government has evolved over time, so has the nature of its elections. Before we begin analyzing them, let's take a brief break from the present and climb into our time machines, back to the birthplace of democracy itself.

The year is 400 B.C.E. in Athens, Greece. You awaken from your relatively peaceful slumber to a commotion outside your front door. Yawning, you roll over in bed and recognize the source of the din outside. It's Election Day, and crowds are already slowly making their way towards the city center. Throwing on a tunic (or something of the kind, forgive my lack of Greek historical knowledge), you exit your front door and push your way through the crowd. A few moments later, you arrive at the center of the city.

Large clay jars have been set in the middle of the public square, and public officials are passing out small black and white pebbles to onlookers. They explain that a white pebble represents a "yes" vote, while a black pebble represents a "no" vote. Another public official reads out the issue being voted on, as decided by a council of 500 randomly selected Athenians. Voters, only free men who have completed their military service, are invited to cast their pebbles into one of the jars, which was later broken apart to tally the vote.[22] You look at the pebbles in your hand (unless, of course, you're not a man who's served in the military), one light and one dark, and decide to cast a "yes" vote, dropping the white pebble into the jar. However, the man behind you is a little bit more undecided. He looks from pebble to pebble, shakes his head, and lets both fall to the ground unceremoniously. As he turns to leave the crowd, one of the public officials grabs his shoulder and implores him to make a decision. The man shakes him off and tries to walk away only to be accosted by two more public officials. They ask him to cast his vote once again, and when he refuses, they demand a heavy tax for refusing to cast a ballot. He hands over the money resentfully, but the officials are unrelenting. Before he's allowed to leave, one of the officials takes a glob of red paint and smears it on the man's face. The mark of the indecisive. You hurry away to the rest of your day, eagerly awaiting to hear the results of the election and satisfied with the role you played in it.

Our democratic systems today resemble those of Ancient Greece, but are far from perfect copies. Early democracy was dominated by majority rule, plain and simple. In the original democracy, cohorts of 500 or so randomly selected citizens decided on issues or rules to be voted on, and the success or failure of these initiatives were determined by the will of the people (read: male, veteran landowners) alone. This represents a direct democracy, or a direct rule by the people. Voting was mandatory (for male, veteran landowners), and therefore the rules and regulations of Athens represented the majority, or at least the majority of male, veteran landowners. However, these democracies have all but gone extinct, with their only vestiges remaining in a few Cantons (governmental administrative regions) of Switzerland, which still are considered direct democracies to this day. In contrast, many countries that call themselves democratic today are actually some form of representative democracy, often called Democratic Republics. These "democracies" work by directly electing representatives to a legislative system like a Parliament or Congress. Ideally, if representatives do their job well they're re-elected, and if not they're kicked to the curb. These systems, generally speaking, solve this major problem of direct democracy: *everyone* needs to vote for *everything*, a costly and arduous process. Instead, representatives are meant to symbolize the will of the people who elected them into office without incurring the cost of regular, nationwide voting. However, do these representatives actually succeed in this task?

Putting a U.S.-centric lens back on, it appears at the surface level that representatives might actually be relatively successful. In the United States, representatives win re-election about 90% of the time, with the number hovering close to 95% in recent years. Senators are only marginally less successful, with a recent re-election rate of 85%.[23] However, it's also worthy of notice that as a collective, Congress's actual approval rating falls somewhere around 20%.[24] While Americans overall tend to hate Congress, the numbers seem to indicate that they believe their own representative isn't the problem, at least not to the point that they need to be removed from office. Is this speculation true, or could other forces be at play that artificially prop up incumbents who would otherwise be removed from office?

Let's start with congressional elections, because they make up the vast majority of federal elections. States actually differ a fair amount in how they conduct elections, but one system reigns supreme in the vast majority of states. In every American state except Louisiana (we'll get to you later), Congressional and Senate elections take place in two different stages, the Primary and the General elections. The Primary election, in most cases, pits members of a political party against each other for the right to be nominated as the standard bearer for that party in the General Election. Then, the General election pits each party's standard bearer against each other to determine a winner. You might recognize this system from the previous chapter on Collective Action. One thing that it accomplishes relatively well is that it allows parties to choose candidates that are palatable to the majority of the party, and will have the largest amount of party support in the general election. However, this system often blocks out candidates from smaller parties, who simply can't compete in a 1:1 matchup with the major parties. Candidates who emerge from these types of elections are often partisan, as their allegiances lie with the party that first nominated them. In winning the party's nomination, they have also gained access to the financial incentives that come with being a standard bearer of a major party (you know those annoying fundraising emails you constantly receive each election season? Most of the money collected from that goes here), and often build up a quick fundraising advantage against future primary and general election opponents. In these systems, it's relatively easy for a candidate who once won a party's nomination to do so again in the future, provided they perform well enough for the party's standards. Even if the candidate doesn't perform as well, this financial advantage still gives them a head start over potentially more qualified challengers. Not to mention, of course, the fact that voters like to win, and are more willing to "bet" on supporting a candidate that's had a history of winning in the past.

In 45 of the 50 states, this is how elections work. Still, there are some interstate differences in determining who is actually allowed to vote in primaries. About half of these states have some version of what's called a closed or partially-closed primary, where only members of a political party are allowed to vote in that party's primary. However, the other half use open or partially-open primaries, where anyone (even sometimes members of the opposing party) has the ability to vote in whatever primary they choose, provided they vote in only one.[25] As could be expected, each method allows voters and candidates a slightly different political calculus in determining who to vote for and what issues to base their campaign on. Candidates running in closed primaries can afford to be slightly more partisan, at least until the general election, as they know that their voters will exclusively be members of their own party. However, in Open primaries, candidates have to consider the possibility that voters might not necessarily support the majority of their policies.

Voters in these states also have a slightly different calculation to make. Often, in swing states or states that are overwhelmingly in favor of a voter's political ideology, people will choose to vote in the party primary that best represents their views, so as to promote a particular candidate they like most. However, in states that constantly elect candidates that run counter to a voter's political ideology (like Alabama to a Democrat or California to a Republican), voters might realize that their candidate of choice has little to no chance of actually winning. In this environment, a voter could "switch sides" and vote in the primaries for the candidate in the opposing party that is the most palatable to them. That way, even if the other party wins, there's more of a chance that the winner will have at least some similar policy priorities to the voter, rather than a candidate that runs completely counter to them. If you happen to live in a state whose politics contradict your political views, this could potentially be a good tactic if your state has open primaries. Even if your state has closed primaries, you could also simply register as a member of the opposing party and vote for the primary candidate that doesn't leave quite as bad of a taste in your mouth.

While this partisan system occurs in the majority of American states, this leaves five other states that buck the trend. These outliers are California, Washington, Louisiana, Nebraska, and Alaska. As California and Washington share the same system, we'll start with them. Rather than holding a primary divided along partisan lines, these western states hold what's called a "Top Two" primary. In this system, every single candidate running for office does so on the exact same ballot. Democrats, Republicans, Libertarians, Greens, Constitutionalists, Socialists, and all other parties compete for the same nominations at the same time. After the first round of voting, the two candidates with the most votes advance to the second round, in which they compete head to head to determine a winner.

Louisiana's primary system works incredibly similarly, and is called a "Jungle Primary" by its proponents. In their system, all candidates similarly compete against each other, however, if one candidate receives over 50% of the vote, there is no run-off (second round) election and that candidate is immediately declared the winner. Nebraska's process works similarly to the Top Two primary, but holds the distinction of being nonpartisan, with no member of their legislature technically belonging to any political party.[16] Alaska probably has the most distinct primary process. They hold primaries that aren't divided by party, similar to the other four, but their process of elimination is rather novel.

Alaska uses a system called Ranked Choice Voting, in which all candidates running for a particular position are on the same ballot. However, instead of voting for one candidate, Alaskan voters rank the candidates from one (favorite) to five (fifth favorite). First, all of the "one" votes are tallied. If a candidate reaches a plurality (50%) of the vote, the election ends and that candidate is declared the winner. If not, then every candidate outside of the top four vote-getters is eliminated. Then, all of the "two" votes from the eliminated candidates are tallied and added to the totals of the top four. Again, if a candidate reaches a plurality, the election is over and that candidate wins. If not, the fourth place candidate is eliminated and their "three" votes are allocated to the top three. This process continues until a candidate has accumulated over 50% of the vote.[25,26]

Apart from the primary process, the actual method of determining a winner can also differ by state. Many states use one of two methods: "plurality rule" and "majority rule." Elections with majority rule require a candidate to win 50% of the vote, while plurality rule, also known as "first-past-the-post," only requires a candidate to beat out their competitors. These two types of electoral counting methods are used differently depending on the type of primary or general election. Top 2 primaries and Jungle primaries often prefer some sort of majority due to their competitive nature. Jungle primaries often have tens of candidates running against each other, and some form of runoff or secondary election is necessary to ensure that candidates don't win after only receiving votes from a very small proportion of the population. The general elections following closed primaries, on the other hand, often don't require such incentives. The general election is often contested by two majority party candidates and a few minority party candidates who may only gather a couple percentage points each, and it's not uncommon for such elections to have a winner who receives over 50% of the vote anyway. As you can probably imagine, minor party candidates often fare better in elections requiring a plurality, as the chances of a minor party candidate reaching the 50% majority necessary in majority vote elections are often slim to none.

There's also another, less commonly used election system that has recently been receiving more national attention. This system is called Ranked Choice Voting, and you already got a bit of a teaser for it in the section before on Alaska. As of 2022, Ranked Choice Voting (RCV) is only used statewide in Alaska and Maine, but it's also been adopted by over 50 cities throughout the U.S. for local elections. Ranked Choice Voting has started to gain traction for a few reasons. First of all, elections are expensive to run, and automatically tracking the multiple preferences of voters reduces the need for holding future runoff elections, allowing runoffs to essentially be conducted as needed directly after the election itself. Additionally, RCV allows voters to have just a little bit more agency in the election process. For those of you who have voted in the past, I'm sure that there's been a time or two when there's been more than one candidate that you feel would do a good job in a particular position. Ranked Choice Voting allows voters to indeed cast ballots for multiple candidates, not only allowing their votes to count for the multiple candidates they would be okay with, but also allowing voters to distance themselves from less palatable candidates by ranking them lower or leaving them off the ballot entirely. Additionally, this system in particular often leads to more palatable candidates winning overall, as candidates need to appeal to a wide variety of voters in order to reach the 50% threshold. In nonpartisan RCV elections, candidates with more polarizing views might gain the number one choice of more polarized voters, but in order to actually win the election, candidates must appeal to voters across the ideological spectrum in order to gain their second, third, forth, and even fifth votes that could actually put them over the edge. For those of you who hope to support or increase the representation of third parties, there's actually some evidence out of Australia that this system can increase the vote totals of third party candidates, as their proponents are able to rank them first without feeling like they could be wasting their vote on a candidate with no chance of winning.[27] RCV would eliminate the idea of "spoiler" candidates, or third party candidates that might reduce the chances of a major party from winning. A more recent example of this was the theory that Jill Stein and Gary Johnson, of the Green and Libertarian parties respectively, might have taken more votes from Hillary Clinton than Donald Trump in 2016 and helped him ascend to the presidency. Ranked Choice Voting could eliminate this tendency, as third party proponents would still likely put major party candidates somewhere on their ballot, allowing them to prioritize their preferred candidate while reducing fears of spoiling the election should their preferred candidate not win.

Additionally, this voting system could actually facilitate cleaner, less contentious elections. As candidates now need to campaign to wider audiences, it becomes harder and harder to get away with bashing another candidate for political gain, as voters might be unsympathetic to such tendencies. In a one on one race, that tactic might work well with enough partisan support behind the candidate (and enough antipathy towards their opponent), but in Ranked Choice Voting, it might cause voters to rank a candidate with similar politics but a better disposition higher, or even leave the offender off the ballot entirely.

However, Ranked Choice Voting doesn't come without its drawbacks. Opponents of the system point to its sometimes confusing nature, and voters indeed can be prone to only voting for one candidate. The money saved from not running additional elections can be offset by a need to educate the public on how the process works. Also, voting for multiple candidates requires more research prior to entering the voting booth, a strategy that should be good for maintaining an informed electorate, but one that doesn't exactly always play out at the ballot box. If individuals vote incorrectly, such as only voting for one candidate, election officials could be left in the difficult position of never having a candidate achieve a plurality, particularly if one is required.

For the first part of this chapter, we've been focusing on Congressional elections, as they make up the vast majority of federal elections in the United States. However, that leaves out what would likely be considered the most important job application in America: the election of the President. This nomination and election process is rather different than any election at the state or local level, so it should largely be examined on its own. Luckily, this is the electoral process that individuals are the most familiar with, but it is also one of the most complicated, so let's dive right in.

First, it's important to note that the presidential election is divided into three separate stages. Two of them you've likely heard of, the primaries and the general election. However, due to the sheer importance of the role of the president, there's a third separate, but rather important, filter applied to the process. This is known as the "Shadow Primary." This somewhat menacing name refers to the period of time before candidate announcement speeches even begin and the official primaries. All 100% of it occurs before a vote has even been cast. During this period of time, presidential hopefuls form exploratory committees, seek out potential donors, and meticulously plan out possible campaign announcement dates to maximize their momentum heading into the primaries. Rather than votes being cast, donations from constituents are used to track the viability of candidates, and polling from the first few states to hold primaries each election cycle (traditionally Iowa and New Hampshire) indicates whether this viability could translate to victories in the future. This is arguably the most important part of the primaries, as it can make or break a candidate's future prospects before a single vote is cast. Indeed, before the first Democratic Primary of the 2020 cycle was held on February 3rd, 18 out of the 29 major candidates running for president had already announced their candidacy and subsequently dropped out due to lack of funding and interest before anyone had a chance to vote for or against them.[28] The potential embarrassment of receiving barely any votes in the primary seems to be enough to filter out less promising candidates at the earliest stage possible.

In addition to fundraising and early campaigning, this shadow primary is often when the debates begin. The presidential debates in particular serve a few different purposes. First and foremost, they allow candidates to stake out their policy positions and make their case to the general public. Second, they force candidates to become clearer about their stances on potentially divisive issues (or at least give a slimy response that doesn't actually answer the question), allowing voters to sort between the candidates they mostly agree and disagree with. Third, the debates are one of the best ways to display the exact sort of temperament that a candidate will take with them to the office of the president. Candidates that go on attack in the primaries will be more likely to do so in a general election or as president, while candidates that avoid the fray and focus on policy will likely do the same in the Oval Office.

Debates are the next major hurdle on a candidate's path to the presidency, and good or bad performances can be beneficial or detrimental to their chances.

While debates play a role throughout the primary process, attention shifts to the primaries themselves after only the first few debates. In theory, the primary process looks very similar to the presidential elections. Candidates who win particular states win certain allocations of electors (or delegates in this case), and the candidate with over 50% of the electors gets nominated. However, the primary process differs from the presidential elections in a few important ways. First, candidates are sometimes (depending on the party and the state) allocated delegates based on the percentage of votes they receive in a state, rather than the pure winner-take-all system of the presidency. Second, the Democratic Party makes use of Superdelegates (I'm not joking, I promise. They're real), a group of super special party officials who aren't pledged to any candidate at all, regardless of who wins the state. Third, the primaries take place over several months, with states' primaries happening on different days.

One factor that plays a much larger role in primary elections is the concept of momentum. In presidential elections, momentum is a one-time thing. The candidate with the most political momentum on election day will likely overperform, and the other will likely underperform. Of course, the role of momentum on election day has been dulled ever so slightly with the increased usage of mail-in voting weeks before votes are counted. In the primary system, political momentum is something that ebbs and flows over time, with debate performances, primary results, and candidate missteps helping to propel some candidacies and sink others. Candidates must keep momentum throughout the many month process in order to win, not only keeping the spotlight on them, but also ensuring that the spotlight casts them in a favorable light. Also, the order of states is particularly important. Traditionally, Iowa and New Hampshire have been the first two states in both parties' primaries, allowing them to set the tone for the rest of the primaries as well as boost (or dampen) candidate momentum. Winning Iowa and New Hampshire can provide a huge boost to a candidate's fortunes, and increase their chances of winning the nomination. Be that as it may, this isn't always the case, as Joe Biden placed fourth and fifth in the Iowa Caucus and New Hampshire Primary, respectively.

However, this tradition has recently come into question in the Democratic party, as having these two states first leads to a not-very-representative population having a disproportionate effect on the rest of the primaries. Namely, both states have a population that is over 90% caucasian, while the United States as a whole is only 60%.

It's worth taking a moment to briefly explain the difference between a primary and a caucus. Keep in mind, in this chapter we'll be talking about strictly presidential election primaries and presidential election caucuses. These, of course, differ from other sorts of primaries (like those that nominate potential congresspeople, senators, and governors). Anyway, both presidential primaries and presidential caucuses are used concurrently to vote for presidential Primary candidates, but each process is slightly different.

Presidential primaries most closely resemble general elections, as voters cast a private ballot to signal their candidate of choice. Presidential Primaries often consist of only one round, and delegates are awarded proportionally to each candidate (except for those pesky superdelegates, whose loyalties aren't revealed until nomination time at the party Convention).

Caucuses, on the other hand, are more of a public event. Caucuses are often divided into different rounds, in which voters physically separate into parts of an area (say, a high school gym) to indicate which candidate they will vote for. After the first round, voters have a chance to physically move and cast their vote for another candidate if they believe that their original candidate has no chance of winning. This can occur several times, and some caucuses require the winner to achieve a certain percentage of the vote, but not always. After the final vote (physical rearrangement of voters), delegates are awarded proportionately as well. Except for the superdelegates, of course, who are determined by party officials at the convention.

After all of the primaries and caucuses have been completed, and all of the delegates have been awarded, hopefully one candidate has reached 50% of the vote. If so, at the party's convention, that candidate is declared the party's nominee for president. If not, the party has a problem, and a "brokered convention" occurs. This process loosely resembles a caucus, except now the delegates pledged to a particular candidate are "released" and can now vote for a different candidate. The process of voting and rearranging continues indefinitely until, finally, a candidate breaks the 50% mark. That candidate is then declared the nominee, and goes on to face the other parties' nominees in the general election.

Now, let's jump forward in time from the primary election to the general. As mentioned before, general elections loosely resemble primary elections, except for the fact that each state's selected candidate receives every single elector pledged to the state, and that the entire election occurs during the exact same period. So, how are numbers of electors determined per state? The process is loosely based on population, but it consists of adding up a state's number of representatives and senators. Each state's number of representatives is based on population (with states receiving roughly one elector per 750,000 people), but two senators are allocated to each state regardless of population. Due to this, smaller states receive a disproportionately large percentage of the vote when compared to larger states, as their number of senators + representatives greatly exceeds the representation that would be deemed "fair" if representation was based on population alone. For example, the state of Wyoming has a population of 579,000, which means it makes up about 0.17% of the US population of 330 million. However, in the electoral college, it receives three out of the 538 votes in the electoral college (two senators + one representative), meaning the state makes up 0.55% of the electoral college, and with that their votes count for almost three times more than the national average. If you feel like this feels slightly unfair, one possible solution to this is referred to as the National Popular Vote Interstate Compact, which would have states distribute electors to different candidates proportionally, similar to how the primary system already works. Either way, once a candidate has won enough states to gain a majority, or 270 of the 538 possible electors, that candidate is declared the new president of the United States. If no candidate reaches the 270 threshold, the election is immediately decided by dividing the House of Representatives into the 50 different states they represent, and giving each state delegation one vote. Then, the Senate elects the vice president.

At this point in time, I would like to pivot from the structure of elections themselves to propose a three part framework for what indeed makes a successful primary and general election candidate, at least from the electorate's perspective in terms of who could actually win an election. The three factors I would like to propose are viability, similarity, and visibility. These factors are certainly not the only ones involved in determining who will emerge the victor, but I believe that these three factors encompass the vast majority of the major elements that allow a candidate to achieve success. Additionally, I would like to clarify that these ideas are based on observation and research, not on exhaustive experimentation. In order to truly prove whether these three factors are all-encompassing, they must experimentally hold up to scrutiny in future elections (to any research-based political scientists reading this who wish to verify this, hello!), otherwise I run the risk of just cherry picking data to fit my hypothesis. Ideally, at least, the candidate who is able to balance all three parts of the framework should achieve the most success in a primary and general election.

Let's start with viability, as it is evident at the earliest point during a political campaign. Viability simply refers to the ability of a primary candidate's campaign to survive long enough to win a general election contest. In order to do so, the candidate must be able to demonstrate that they are able to financially support a potential victory in both a primary election and the later general election campaign. Viability often becomes apparent early on during the shadow primary. Even if a candidate is the most gifted orator and persuader in the world, their presidential campaign requires a huge investment of time and money to actually turn out voters at the ballot box. Remember, presidential candidates need to attempt to appeal to over 330 million people spread out across almost four million square miles of territory. While the internet and social media has made this task slightly easier, it's also even easier now for well-funded candidates to block the airwaves from their cash-strapped competitors. Therefore, if a presidential candidate hopes to succeed, they must show that they're able to fund a campaign from start to finish.

Using the 2020 democratic primary as a model, let's look at two possible options for how to do so. The first of these we'll refer to as the Bloomberg method. Michael Bloomberg is a billionaire and former mayor of New York City who entered the 2020 Democratic primary after the official primaries had begun. Completely skipping the shadow primary, he mostly self-funded his campaign, overruling any questions of viability. This strategy proved to be only somewhat successful, as he ended the Democratic primary with the fourth most delegates, but only succeeded in winning American Samoa outright. His viability allowed him to evade the pitfalls of the shadow primary completely, but didn't allow him to come close to winning the nomination. Another possible route to viability is exhibited by Bernie Sanders. The Sanders method, for example, focused on making the campaign as much of a grassroots movement as possible. Throughout the primaries, Sanders raised more money than any other candidate, but also received among the smallest average donations and had the most individual donors. [29,30] This strategy is likely more powerful than the Bloomberg method, as a combination of small dollar donations from lots of individual voters is indicative of potential future support. If someone is willing to donate to a candidate, they're likely to vote for them in the future. However, other factors must certainly be at play as well, seeing as Bernie Sanders finished second in the primary to 46th president Joe Biden.

The second part of this framework refers to similarity. This metric refers to how similar a particular candidate's policy preferences are to the preferences of the individuals likely to vote for them. Similarity, unfortunately, is much harder to directly measure than viability, as voter preferences are often more complicated than their identity as liberal or conservative. Most people don't directly fall on party lines, and often have at least a couple of opinions that are distributed widely across the political spectrum. When we talk about political identities, it's important to try to speak in aggregates, but not absolutes. The vast majority of Democrats are liberal. The vast majority of Republicans are conservative. However, there are certainly somewhat conservative Democrats and somewhat liberal Republicans and, additionally, due to the two-party system, voters who would generally become part of a Socialist, Libertarian, or Christian Democratic party (and so many others) in another country often find themselves folded into the Democratic or Republican party in the USA. However, at the macro level, there are certain trends that occur so that candidates can attempt to ensure that they are as similar to their potential voters as possible.

Political parties are more polarized than the general electorate. So, when candidates are attempting to win a primary, it makes sense for them to aim for the political center of the party lines, so they can gather as wide of a coalition within the party as possible. One recent notable exception would likely be that of a certain Bernie Sanders, who occupied the left wing of the Democratic party almost to himself, beating out candidates in a crowded Center (and remaining in first place in the delegate count) until enough had dropped out to consolidate support around a certain moderate Joe Biden, who eventually won the primary handily. Most candidates run more politically polarized campaigns during the primaries, then take a hard turn towards the center to court more moderate voters upon advancing to the general election. This has been the conventional move for a while now, but was recently called into question by a couple of presidential elections. This wisdom seemed to hold true until 2016, when Republican nominee Donald Trump didn't make a hard left turn towards the center after winning the Republican primary. Traditionally, the definition of similarity has centered around an ability to rally support around an already similar base, while simultaneously convincing undecideds to believe the candidate is similar enough to themselves to vote for them. However, Trump upended this conventional choice in 2016, and almost did again in 2020, by focusing his messaging specifically towards his base voters. It appears that Trump was able to make the calculation that the same message that appealed towards his primary voters (and caused them to turn out en masse on election day) would indeed appeal enough to a general election audience, and at least in 2016, he might have been correct. After all, he enjoyed a similar but converse populist appeal on the Right to that of Bernie on the Left, and won the shadow primary in terms of number of donors as well as money raised. To a similar degree, in 2020, Joe Biden ran a primary campaign that could be argued to be to the right of many democratic base voters, and still was able to secure the nomination and eventually the presidency. However, Biden also benefited from a perceived increase in viability, as many Democratic voters believed that he would have the best chance of defeating Donald Trump, an assumption that seems to have been proved correct. It appears that similarity might not necessarily be determined by the concepts of "left" vs "right" anymore, and that something else, such as populist sentiment, might come into play as well. It will be interesting to watch future primary elections to see if this new trend holds, or if the structure of primaries reverts back to what it looked like previously.

Third, I propose the concept of visibility as a potential factor in determining candidate success. Visibility, in this instance, refers almost completely to the concept of name recognition. It's a simple fact that the majority (upwards of 80 or 85% by some metrics[31]) follow politics either casually or not at all. As you know, one of the main purposes of this book is to change that. However, many people don't have a choice in terms of how much they follow politics. Most are rightfully focused on putting food on the table, and paying close attention to politics can often seem like a luxury afforded to those rich in time and resources. Unfortunately, this leads to the electorate sometimes picking candidates that they simply know something about, and believe could do a reasonably decent job running the country. Due to this, some candidates who might theoretically make better presidents can become overlooked simply because they're not widely known. For example, before the 2020 primaries, candidates Joe Biden, Bernie Sanders, and Elizabeth Warren had the widest name recognition among the electorate, in that order.[32] It's somewhat unsurprising, then, that these three candidates ended up in first, second, and third in the Democratic primary. Similarly, former president Donald Trump had the highest name recognition in the 2016 Republican primary.[33] Are elections therefore doomed to be simply contests of name recognition? Well, if we go back a little bit further, we run into a young liberal firebrand, presidential candidate Barack Obama. While polling before the 2008 election is somewhat harder to find, Obama clearly fell behind frontrunner Hillary Clinton in name recognition.[34] However, disputes about Clinton's likeability and electability led to Barack Obama securing the nomination. What he lacked in name recognition was made up for by his viability in a general election, as well as being similar enough to the Electorate. Still, I believe it's worth noticing that some concerns about Clinton's likeability seemed to fall to the background in 2016, when she was likely going to face a similarly dislikeable candidate, Donald Trump.

If you look back to see the winners of the most recent presidential elections, you'll see a trend that these winners managed to win two out of these three metrics throughout the primaries and the general election. During the 2016 primaries, Donald Trump maintained viability, similarity to his base, and visibility, while Hillary Clinton's viability began to drop off with an increase in large dollar donations (indicating the support of wealthier donors, rather than grassroot support) and the timing of the Comey report, which put Clinton's ethics in question at the 11th hour. In the 2020 election, Biden capitalized on his viability and visibility, and eventually defeated Donald Trump due to increased viability (as determined by donations) and similarity to the general electorate. While all three are not always completely necessary, it seems likely that maintaining a lead in 2 of these metrics throughout both the primary and general elections puts a candidate on the path towards achieving victory.

Unfortunately, a candidate's quality alone often isn't enough to ensure victory, especially outside of presidential elections. The best candidate doesn't always win. To explore this a little bit more, we're going to shift back to America's Congress, to the House of Representatives in particular. At this point in time, you're probably pretty familiar with the ways in which representatives are elected into office. However, what we haven't gotten into yet is exactly who represents who. You see, determining this in the Senate is significantly easier. Each state receives two senators, and each senator is voted into office by and represents the entire population of the state they ran for office in. But the House of Representatives works a little bit differently. If you remember, representatives are allocated to states proportionally, according to the population of each state. This means that each state has an incredibly variable number of representatives, from the 53 representatives of California (the most populous state) to the aforementioned one representative of Wyoming (the least populous state). As the House of Representatives was designed to be more responsive to its constituents than the Senate, a concept that is elucidated in the chapter on the Legislative branch, the areas representatives represent had to be significantly reduced in size. Rather than having representatives attempt to determine the needs of the entire state, it was decided that each representative would be beholden to a particular chunk of the state's population, an electoral district, none more or less populous than the others. Through a process called redistricting, state legislatures would draft and certify district maps, often subject to gubernatorial (governor's) veto power.[35]

What quickly began to occur was that the party in power would not only draw state districts that favored their own party in the state legislatures, but they would draw congressional districts that would benefit their party in the national House of Representatives as well. One of the earliest examples of this starts with a certain Massachusetts governor named Elbridge Gerry. During his tenure as Governor, Gerry signed into law a congressional district map that included a rather misshapen district that cut certain counties into pieces, diluting the power of the Federalist-aligned regions in favor of his own party, the Democratic-Republicans. Opponents of this map noticed that this particular district represented (the mythical version of) a Salamander, and thus, the GerryMander was born:

Wikimedia Commons

Today, salamanders are real creatures that look very little like the mythical version above, but either way, the name has stuck. Gerrymandering has remained a prominent feature of America's system since. First and foremost, we need to understand that this practice works simply as a function of keeping a particular political party in power as long as possible. Gerrymandering occurs both on the state and national level, and the parties deciding where district lines are drawn are often the ones who directly benefit from how the lines are drawn. By design, gerrymandering is a partisan and antidemocratic institution that attempts to dilute the power of certain groups of people while increasing the power of others. So, how exactly does it work?

Before we look at an example in real life, it might be a good idea to start with a more clear-cut example. Suppose we have a "state" with 50 different precincts, or for our purposes, let's just say 50 different voters. Each voter is a member of either the Gray party or the White party. This particular state has been allocated five congresspeople, and therefore these 50 voters need to be divided into five equally sized groups. There are multiple ways to do so, but some of the most common are shown below:

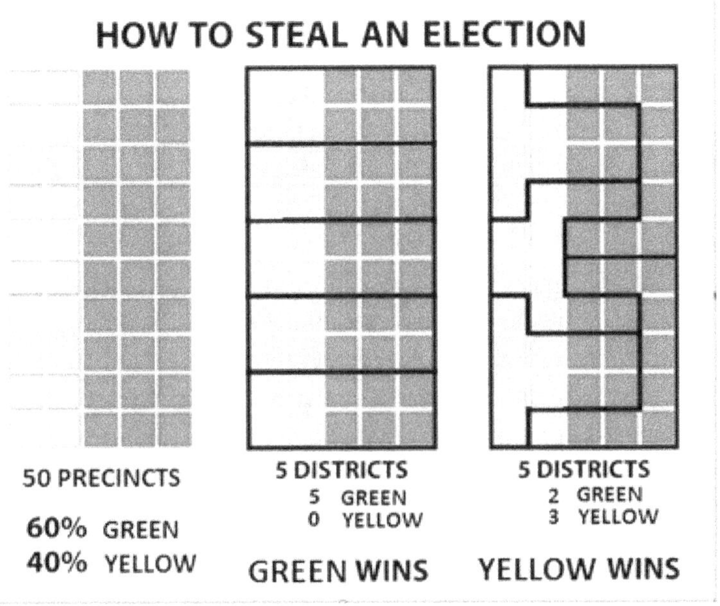

Wikimedia Commons[37]

The first example represents direct, or proportional, representation. When directly counted, 60% of voters represent the Gray party, while 40% of voters represent the White party. If we drew congressional districts to match this proportional representation, we could draw five vertical districts, one along each column of voters. In this case, the 60% to 40% split remains the same, with the Gray party sending three members to congress, while the White party sends the other two.

The second example represents a rather excellent (if disingenuous) example of gerrymandering from the Gray party. Rather than dividing the voters vertically, the Grays decided to divide them into two separate horizontal rows. Because of this, even though the population proportions remain the same at 60% to 40%, the Gray party gets to send all five members to congress, while the White party gets shut out from sending any. This particular example of gerrymandering is particularly ingenious, because at first glance it doesn't *look* like gerrymandering. After all, the Gray party simply laid out five horizontal districts of the same shape and size, what could be fairer than that? The true guile lies in the results of the gerrymander, rather than simply what the districts look like.

The third example, however, represents a rather clever gerrymander from the White party. Instead of dividing any of the districts evenly, the White party decides to force the vast majority of Gray voters into two incredibly Gray-heavy districts, while the White party maintains a slim majority in the other three districts. While the White party only has 40% of voters in this state, due to their gerrymandering practices they are able to send three members to congress, while the "majority" Gray party only gets to send two.

While this is a visually appealing explanation, lines often become slightly more blurry when actually put into practice. Voting tendencies aren't as clear as just White and Gray, and while likeminded people tend to aggregate, the political divides in a state are just a bit more complicated than just squares in a chart. Let's take a particular state as an example. I grew up in Kansas, so that is the state I'm most familiar with. We also only have four congressional districts, which along with our semi-rectangular shape, makes our congressional map (as of 2022) one of the easier ones to understand.

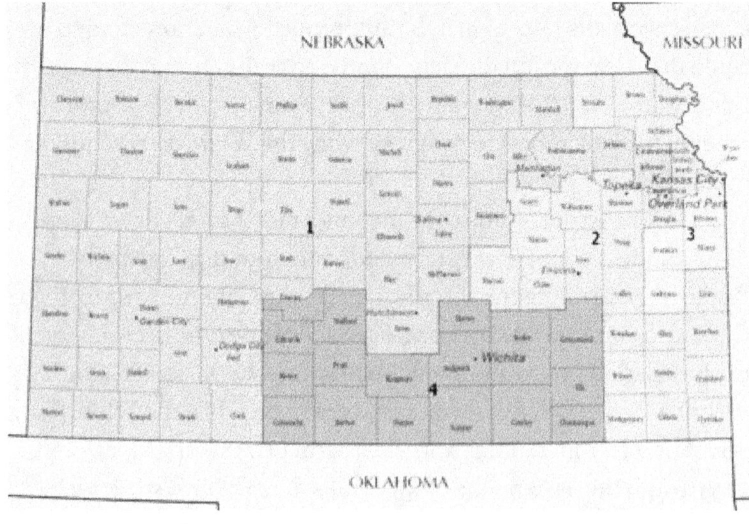

Wikimedia Commons[38]

Kansas has six major cities approaching or exceeding 100,000 individuals: Wichita, Kansas City, Overland Park (a suburb of Kansas City), Olathe, Topeka, and Lawrence.[36] All of these cities (minus Olathe, which lies Southwest of Overland Park) can be seen overlaid by the congressional district map above. Additionally, these cities lean Democratic except for Wichita, which is incredibly moderate but sometimes leans Republican. Due to this leaning, the Kansas State Congress's Republican majority has an incentive to draw maps that increase the amount of districts that lean Republican, and decrease the amount that lean Democratic. In order to do this, the party in power (in this case the Republicans) hopes to draw as many Republican districts as possible, diluting Democratic power as much as possible. The current map does this by isolating or even bisecting cities such as Kansas City, Overland Park, Topeka, and Lawrence into districts one, two, and three, while pairing them with large swaths of Rural, Republican-leaning territory, likely dividing Kansas into four separate Republican districts. However, it's notable that in this case, Democrat Sharice Davids won re-election in the third district. Much of this likely has to do with the fact that Kansas currently has a progressive leaning Supreme Court and a Democratic governor, both of whom provide counterweights against the vast Republican majority in the state legislature and have ruled previous overly-gerrymandered maps unconstitutional.

Even though Gerrymandering was technically deemed illegal by the Supreme Court case Davis v. Bandemer, the Court unfortunately did not set a standard for what gerrymandering actually looks like in practice, making it incredibly difficult for gerrymandered maps to be struck down by the courts.[39] Because of this, the majority of state legislatures continue to gerrymander relatively freely, only occasionally being struck down by a court ruling or vetoed by a governor of the opposing party, measures that really only serve as slaps on the wrist, and result in only slightly less gerrymandered maps passing on the next attempt.

Unfortunately, it appears that one of the only ways to truly stop partisan gerrymandering is from a political practice almost unheard of in this era: kneecapping one's own political power for the common good. However, a surprising amount of states have decided to make that exact move. Rather than trusting redistricting practices to the state legislature, a total of nine states have made the decision to allow a non-politician, nonpartisan commission to draw their congressional maps. Since they deserve plaudits for making this move, the aforementioned nine states are as follows: Washington, Idaho, Montana, California, Arizona, Colorado, Hawaii, Michigan, and New Jersey. Additionally, New York and Virginia use a hybrid system, allowing a nonpartisan commission to draw the maps, while the state legislature has some say on corrections.[40] These nonpartisan commissions represent one way to reduce the amount of gerrymandering occurring in our elections, and are likely one of the most important steps that America has taken towards improving our democracy in recent years. Still, remember that the majority of states still either explicitly or implicitly practice some form of gerrymandering, diluting the power of minority groups across America in favor of often homogenous majorities. If America seeks to improve the validity and representativeness of its elections, solving the problems caused by gerrymandering would be a fantastic place to start.

Chapter 5: The Executive Branch

President. Head of State. Commander in Chief. Leader of the Free World. The numerous appellations of the position makes very apparent the political, military, and social power that this individual holds. However, when America's founders first determined how the country would be run, power was the last thing on their minds. The newly created United States had just won the Revolutionary War, and sought first and foremost to avoid creating a government led by royalty who governed unilaterally with little regard for, or reprimand from, the people their decrees impacted. So, the United States got rid of it. On November 15th, 1777, the Continental Congress, with representatives from each newly created state, finally settled on a form of government. Rather than a central leader, these Articles of Confederation established a unicameral (with only one house of legislature, rather than the current two) Congress to "make war and peace; conduct foreign affairs; request men and money from the states; coin and borrow money; regulate Indian affairs; and settle disputes among the states."[41] All other powers were to be reserved to the states, who were to be united by a "league of friendship." Friendship bracelets aside, the new U.S. government figured out that completely curtailing the power of the Federal Government wasn't exactly the best idea. The government had no power to raise revenue through taxation nor curtail inflation, and even though they gave themselves power to settle interstate disputes, their decisions were more of friendly pushes in the right direction than legal frameworks. Much of this came to a head in the summer of 1786, in the countryside of Massachusetts.

While the Federal Government wasn't given the power to tax, the state governments absolutely could. As many of the states went into a fair amount of debt following the Revolutionary War, it became rather difficult to perform many of the functions a government needs to perform in order to adequately survive. So, the state of Massachusetts did what any cash-strapped government with few other options could do: tax its citizens. Unfortunately, many of the individuals they were taxing were the same Revolutionary War soldiers that they were unable to adequately pay for their wartime service, due to the aforementioned war debt. You can see how this quickly became a problem for Massachusetts. Daniel Shays, a Continental Army Captain who was more than just a little concerned about the fact that he was still being taxed (and not paid) by the government he had fought for against another government that had also highly taxed him, as well as the fact that the same government was taking legal action against its people through debtors' courts, decided to stage a rebellion in order to fix the problem. Together with other former soldiers, he and his band of merry men attacked courthouses and government properties (as well as anyone who defended them) around Massachusetts, gathering support from other insurgents along the way. The rebellion continued in spurts until it finally culminated at the Springfield Arsenal the next January, where Shays and his men were finally stopped by military forces before breaching the Arsenal and gaining control of the weapons inside. After a skirmish, Shays and 12 members of his militia were captured and condemned to death by the State of Massachusetts. However, many of the rebels, including Shays himself, were pardoned the following year and Shays ended up receiving a pension for his service in the Revolutionary War. [42,43]

Shays' Rebellion proved to be the last straw for the Articles of Confederation, as it made abundantly clear that the Articles were too weak to stand on their own. However, the original problem leading to the American Revolution in the first place still remained.

How could this new government have enough power to regulate trade, raise money, stop rebellions, and perform all other duties necessary for survival, but also ensure that said government doesn't abuse those powers to the detriment of its people? In order to do so, a constitutional convention was called for, bringing together representatives from each state (except for Rhode Island, who refused to validate a more powerful Federal Government by sending representatives) to attempt to solve the problem. The delegates decided to first try to amend the Articles of Confederation, however, they discovered that the majority of the document would need to be scrapped and they would have to begin anew. After four months of debate and 10 months to secure ratification from the required nine out of thirteen states, the new Constitution went into effect on June 21st, 1788.[44] The Constitution instituted an Executive and Judicial branch in addition to an amended Legislative branch: three partners in governance with their own individual powers. You see, the institutions of three separate branches of government had multiple different purposes. First, dividing the government in three allowed government officials to specialize in particular areas, allowing them to perform specific roles and not be overwhelmed by legislating, leading, and scrutinizing the Constitution at the same time. However, the most important reason for dividing the government was that of dividing power.

You see, while the Constitutional Convention largely agreed that the scope of government needed to be larger, many were similarly concerned that the branch leading the government could go rogue and take over, making the position similar to that of a king. The Convention tested many different ways of avoiding this, from a president-by-committee to simply drastically reducing the powers of the President and giving them to the other branches, but they kept running up against the problem that not only could a group of people go rogue, but also that governance by a group wouldn't be agile enough to adequately respond to national emergencies like wars, natural disasters, or epidemics. As a result, the Constitutional Convention came up with a solution that has withstood the test of time rather well: the Separation of Powers. Sure, each branch had their own powers, but the other branches had a similar power to keep the others in check.

The Constitution describes the Executive branch, and the President in charge of it, as having several different powers, including making treaties, appointing ambassadors, nominating Supreme Court Justices, serving as the commander in chief of the armed forces, granting pardons, and filling congressional vacancies. These serve as the vast majority of powers explicitly afforded to the Executive branch by the Constitution, and in theory should serve as a guardrail to curtail the powers of the president. Of course, this doesn't often play out as well in reality. Over time, the power of the President has slowly expanded as office holders have ever so gently (and sometimes forcefully) pushed at the boundaries of what the Executive branch can do. One of the more heavy handed approaches to doing so is through the imposition of executive orders. In what might be considered by some to be a cheat code for advancing an administration's goals, an executive order is a President's unilateral decision to make the Executive branch operate a certain way, do a certain thing, or avoid doing another thing. Yes, I know that's incredibly vague, but much of the Constitution is purposefully vague as well, so here we are. An executive order can only be issued by a President, however, the order can also be revoked by a future President, or deemed unconstitutional by the Judicial branch (three cheers for checks and balances).

With this in mind, it's important to additionally know what makes an executive order (EO) constitutional or unconstitutional. While the Constitutionality of an EO might just depend on the ideological balance of the Supreme Court itself, there are some listed rulings that can help us determine which are legal and which are not. While executive orders themselves aren't explicitly mentioned in the Constitution,[45] the Constitution does give the president power over the Executive branch as well as the power to enforce laws as necessary. Even without being mentioned in the Constitution, George Washington issued the first proclamation resembling an executive order, asking department heads to provide "a full, precise, and distinct general idea of the affairs of the United States" they oversaw.[46] This was one of the actions that first established his Cabinet. Always aware of the precedent he was setting, Washington used executive orders sparingly, only issuing eight during his entire presidency. The orders themselves ranged in purpose. A couple were administrative, such as creating a Cabinet or defining the boundaries of Washington, D.C. One, issued on Thursday, November 26th, established the holiday of Thanksgiving and instructed Americans to abide by any treaties made with Native American Tribes. During the Whiskey Rebellion, Washington issued an executive order requiring the rebels to pay the liquor tax that had been imposed on them.[47] As you can see, Washington's first executive orders set the precedent that they should only be used according to the Constitutional guidelines set apart for the Executive branch, and any exceeding these guidelines would be considered unconstitutional. In this sense, EOs can direct parts of the Executive branch to perform (or not perform) particular actions, but in return, these orders should only apply to parts of the Executive branch if they hope to remain Constitutional.

In addition, the number and scope of executive orders issued by presidents has drastically increased over time.[48] While George Washington himself only issued eight during his entire presidency, and the next twelve issued no more than eighteen, recent presidents Donald Trump and Joe Biden are on track to issue several hundred through the course of their terms. However, historically speaking, Trump and Biden would only be considered to be pretty average in terms of the amount of executive orders they've issued. At the top of the list is Franklin Delano Roosevelt, ending with a whopping 3,721 executive orders, averaging more per year than most other presidents passed throughout their entire term.

While many executive orders are simply passed in the first couple days of a presidency to overturn a previous president's executive orders, why was there such a heavy peak during and around FDR's presidency, and a slow reduction since then? One potential explanation is that the number of executive orders could potentially correlate with the degree of problems facing the nation at that particular moment. While this doesn't necessarily hold true for the infancy of the United States, the number of EO's begins to pick up in the years during and after the 1850s, with Abraham Lincoln, Andrew Johnson, and Ulysses S. Grant. Indeed, many of the executive orders issued during this time occurred simultaneously with the Civil War, as well as the Reconstruction Era that directly followed the war. After this time, the number stays relatively stagnant until Theodore Roosevelt bucks the trend and passes a whopping 1,081 executive orders during his term. Roosevelt could potentially prove as an exception to our rule, as Teddy faced no large wars on American soil during his presidency and apart from a rather significant economic panic in 1907, the United States was largely enjoying an era of relative prosperity and economic power on the world's stage. However, it could be argued that Roosevelt's partiality for executive orders was more personal than practical. As President, Teddy Roosevelt wrote: "I did not usurp power, but I did greatly broaden the use of executive power." He believed that the office of the president was to be a "steward of the people," that should take "whatever action necessary for the public good unless expressly forbidden by law or the Constitution." [49,50] Clearly, Roosevelt saw the presidency as a mandate to provide for the public good, and he often used executive orders in order to do so, creating the Food and Drug Administration, trust busting by breaking up monopolies, and even establishing the National Parks system to conserve America's wildlife and natural beauty.

Roosevelt's beliefs about the role of the president expanded the powers of the Executive branch, and the presidents immediately following him looked similar in their proportions of executive orders. That is, until a certain Franklin Delano Roosevelt, Teddy's fifth cousin, stepped up to the plate. Executive orders must run in the family. FDR entered office in 1932 in one of the largest landslide victories since George Washington's electoral shutout. Along with this came a mandate to govern, as the massive victory indicated that the public would largely be on his side. In the wake of his landslide,

Roosevelt pledged a New Deal with Americans who had recently been rocked by the Great Depression. He would use a series of fireside chats to lay out his legislative proposals, such as Social Security, wealth taxes, controls over banks, and introduction of the Tennessee Valley Authority to provide power, flood protection, and cheap fertilizer to rural regions.[51] However, it wasn't until the dawn of World War II that FDR was able to fully pull the United States out of the Great Depression, often by creating jobs as soldiers abroad or in weapons manufacturing back at home. It is here where our prediction regarding the reason for an increase in executive orders begins to come to fruition: Not only does FDR have a personal inclination towards using the Federal Government to solve problems at home and abroad, but the poverty caused by the Great Depression and the threat of World War II greatly increased the public's tolerance for a more powerful president, allowing the most executive-order-friendly president to be elected four separate times, the only time this has occurred in the history of the United States.

After Roosevelt, the number of executive orders passed has dwindled down to current levels, with only a brief spike during Bill Clinton's tenure. While one reason for this could be due to a more peaceful, economically sound period of time after World War II, it's possible that other forces are at play, particularly since this period of time has certainly not been without war or economic turmoil. The second reason could be due to the simple replaceability of executive orders. You see, every single executive order issued has a potential expiration date, one that is often reached the moment another president steps into office. While these orders can have considerable powers within the Executive branch, they can be overturned as soon as a different president is installed in the Oval Office. The third possible reason is one that is just a little bit more reassuring. There has been a considerable amount of evidence that passing executive orders may indeed have a negative impact on a president's approval rating.[52] As could probably be expected, Americans aren't exactly the largest fans of a president acting unilaterally, without consent from other branches of government. Therefore, when a president does indeed act unilaterally, there have been documented negative effects on their approval rating, and consequently their chances of being re-elected.

While hopefully the contents of this section have allowed you to make up your mind on whether executive orders fall closer to an abuse of power or a necessary, temporary evil, if you do happen to fall on the side of an abuse of power, you can rest somewhat assured that with enough collective action and public knowledge of the executive order itself, the president in question might just be hammering one more nail into the coffin of their future electoral hopes.

Even though executive orders are one way that presidents can exact control on the Executive branch, the Executive branch in itself may be more or less sympathetic to the president's orders depending on its makeup. You see, this branch itself is the largest of the three by several orders of magnitude, consisting of the President, Vice President, Cabinet Members, and somewhere around three million federal employees, from the DMV to the Postal Service.[53] While presidents attempt to create a Cabinet as favorable to their political agendas as they can, they sometimes don't have as much agency as they would like, as Cabinet member nominations are subject to a majority vote in the Senate before they can be installed into the Federal Government. This is often not a huge concern, as most nominees are confirmed rather easily unless there's a concern regarding their ability to lead, meaning that presidents are often successful in creating a Cabinet that is at least somewhat amenable to their policy goals. But, while these Secretaries and Undersecretaries are often on board with the current president, the millions of federal workers underneath them may not be. The services provided by the majority of these jobs (such as those in post offices and the DMV) aren't affected much whether a liberal or conservative occupies the position. However, this doesn't mean that their positions aren't political, or can't affect the broader political sphere in some way. Take the Postal Service for instance. During his administration, Donald Trump appointed Louis DeJoy, a Republican businessman, to the office of Postmaster General, a position he held well into the Biden administration. During his tenure as Postmaster General, leading up to the 2020 election, DeJoy banned overtime and extra trips to deliver mail, removed 600 high speed mail sorting machines from post offices around the country, and removed mail collection boxes from many cities.[54] While many of these changes could be argued to be cost cutting measures, they also increased the time it took for mail to be delivered leading up to an election that promised more voting by mail than any previous election. With the late appointment to his post, Postmaster DeJoy remained in charge of the Post Office during the Biden administration. Even though his politics puts him firmly against Biden's policy plans, DeJoy legally can't be removed from his post unless he displays "malfeasance or extreme neglect of duty."[55] DeJoy's case demonstrates the amount of agency that individual members of the Executive branch have under the president, indicating that they aren't always perfect purveyors of the president's will, and can sometimes even be actively working against the administration. Of course, the president often has a course of action (i.e. executive orders) to correct the direction of a particular department gone off course; however, this comes with the usual added risk of seeming dictatorial or authoritarian to the electorate. Additionally, certain antipathetic members of the department could choose to drag their feet in enacting these executive orders, reducing their efficacy.

While the political leanings of potential higher up Executive branch officials might have some large, unintended impacts on how departments are run, the same can happen at the lower levels. The Executive branch's charge, at its very core, is to enforce the laws of the United States. In order to do so, an Executive branch uses different mechanisms of enforcement, such as the FBI and CIA, police forces, sheriffs, and a prison system. While some of these organizations and individuals are beholden to the people they represent (such as sheriffs, who are often directly elected by constituents), many are not. Due to this, one's political ideology can play a rather large role in exactly *how* the laws are enforced, if at all.

For a quick example of this at the state level of the Executive branch, let's take a quick trip, so to speak.

A particularly salient example of political ideology affecting the Federal Government's enforcement of laws at the state level is how often drug policies are enforced. While hallucinogens such as LSD, Psilocybin Mushrooms, and others still remain illegal at the state level in all fifty states, marijuana has seen a rapid increase in legality, and it's been estimated that at the time of writing this, roughly 33% of Americans live in a state that has legalized marijuana.[56] As marijuana legalization grew in popularity, numerous police stations where marijuana usage was still illegal turned to a strategy called a Lowest Law Enforcement Priority. This tactic pushed marijuana-related arrests down to the bottom of a police department's list of priorities, meaning that departments would exhaust all other possible criminal activity before moving on to crimes related to marijuana usage and possession.[57] Additionally, some city halls have even put this Lowest Law Enforcement Priority up to a referendum (sometimes colloquially referred to, of course, as a Reeferendum) to let citizens themselves determine law enforcement priorities on this particular subject.

One particularly important and often overlooked feature of the Executive branch is its size. Due to the sheer size of this branch, it's impossible for any president or cabinet official to fully oversee all of its members, and the branch itself relies on an ever-descending web of supervisors and supervisees in order to ensure it is working as intended. This leaves room for public officials at the local level to turn a blind eye to certain directives, due to how difficult oversight is. Of course, here is where the agency of citizens and voters comes into play. If voters are able to sufficiently mobilize public opinion around a certain policy, such as drug reform, even if a state's government can't write it into law, the Executive branch can choose to deprioritize enforcing particular laws that could turn public opinion against them.

In this way, the Executive branch is responsive to public opinion in a much less obvious way than, say, the Legislative branch.

In order to maintain public trust and credibility, the Executive branch, particularly at the local level, needs to be at least somewhat responsive to the needs of its people. If not, it loses a lot of leverage in its ability to enforce the law. Therefore, the Executive branch is responsive to the will of the people in two different ways. Not only are their leaders elected into office, as is the case with mayors, governors, and presidents, but the branch also needs to maintain the trust of its citizens in order to keep some semblance of authority. After all, who would re-elect a public servant they didn't believe was acting in favor of the public good?

Chapter 6: The Legislative Branch

Some of you may remember the good old days of elementary school teachers wheeling a giant, old, portable TV into the room on days that they needed a bit of a break to grade papers, plan lessons, or perhaps recover from a previous night out on the town. One of the programs I remember most viscerally from this time period came from musical education giant Schoolhouse Rock!™ which taught different subjects to students through whimsical, musical short episodes (if you're incredibly confused right now, don't worry, the nostalgia break will be over soon). One of their songs in particular that I heard in elementary school is still burned into my brain today, a particular civics ditty called "I'm Just a Bill," which rather expertly musically depicted the process of a Bill becoming a Law, from Committee all the way to the desk of the President. However, one verse in particular stood out to me:

> "Some folks back home decided they wanted a law passed
> So they called their local Congressman, and he said
> You're right, there oughta be a law.
> Then he sat down
> And wrote me out and introduced me to Congress.
> And I became a bill, and I'll remain a bill
> Until they decide to make me a law." [58]

From "I'm Just a Bill, Schoolhouse Rock!"™

Okay, okay, their rhyme scheme and sense of rhythm wasn't exactly perfect, but it certainly got the job done. Anyway, little Matthew thought it was very cool that any old citizen could come up with an idea that eventually could become a law to improve the entire country! Naturally, when I got home I found the email address of my local congressperson, and offered to them the idea of creating National Kindness Day, a day where everyone was legally required to do something kind for another person. Exactly what happens if someone broke the law, I apparently hadn't figured out yet and, with the benefit of hindsight, being arrested for not being kind sounds like some kind of dystopian nightmare. Naturally, I never heard back, and I decided to forget about National Kindness Day for a while.

Silly backstory aside, it got me thinking about how exactly the government is (or isn't) responsive to the needs of its citizens, as well as how many laws are actually conceived in the minds of constituents. While it's incredibly difficult to ascertain which laws were the brainchildren of citizens vs. those introduced by lobbyists or congresspeople themselves (although I could probably make an educated guess it's overwhelmingly in favor of the latter two), Americans actually are incredibly split on their perceptions of whether ordinary citizens can influence the government. According to 2015 polling by Pew Research, exactly 50% of citizens believe that they can do a lot to influence the government, but only if they work hard enough to do it. The other 50% either don't believe so or don't know.[59] The problem with this, of course, is that both sides are absolutely correct.

If you don't believe that you, as a voter, can influence policy passed by the government, then of course you're never going to succeed in doing so. It's simply a self-fulfilling prophecy at this point. On the other hand, if you do believe that you're going to succeed, you might just have a chance. Fortunately, one of the ways that citizens can actually have some influence on government officials is by simply contacting the ones that are meant to most represent you. While a letter to the president might have the most direct impact, it doesn't take a genius to recognize that the odds of the president reading your carefully written policy proposal are incredibly close to zero. However, the odds of your local congressperson (or, even more so, a state or local government official) reading your carefully written policy proposal are significantly higher, even if they scoff and toss it in the fireplace directly afterwards. Still, the odds of your local lawmaker either reading your proposal or condemning it to a scrap heap depends as much on the *level* of representative they are as it does on the *type* of representative they are. Once you're able to recognize what type of representative your congressperson or senator is, you can better determine their chances of actually acting on pressure from their constituents. Largely, there are three different types of representatives: delegates, trustees, and partisans.[60]

Let's start with delegates. First and foremost, delegates believe that they were elected purely to represent the will of the people that they were elected by. They place the highest importance on the margin that they were elected by, and do a lot of constituent work to determine where their voters stand, and how they can best represent them. They're more likely to stay true to what their constituents want, rather than what the party or country as a whole wants. When it comes down to it, they recognize that the people who put them in office are the ones in their legislative district or state, and these are the ones that matter the most to them in the end. These congresspeople are excellent at actually representing their constituents, but can sometimes appear to stand in the way of national politics, particularly if they take a stance that their constituents agree with that the national environment does not. If you're hoping to have a representative who is actually willing to read your policy proposal and carefully consider it, consider electing a representative who appears to have the qualities of a delegate. However, look out if the local political headwinds change, as their loyalties can be easily swayed.

Trustees, on the other hand, believe that they were elected into Congress by people who *trust* them to make the right decisions. Trustees tend to think that they know what is best for their constituents, and might even believe that they're able to make a better decision because they have more information as a member of Congress. Trustees can find success when their legislative agendas actually do enrich the lives of their constituents, but they can often walk a slippery slope when they appear to know more, but keep passing legislation that their constituents don't agree with that also doesn't appear to enrich their lives. A particularly hardlining trustee likely wouldn't even see your proposal in the first place, as they've probably instructed their staffers to provide a genuine-sounding response before forgetting the proposal ever existed. The views and policy preferences of trustees tend to be pretty stable throughout their times in office, unless they come across information that could potentially render their beliefs incorrect.

Partisans are just about what you would expect, they pledge fealty to the party and to the party alone. They believe that allegiance to a particular party helped them to secure office in the first place, and they need to keep this coalition together in order to win re-election the next time. Often, this strategy is relatively successful (similar to the delegate strategy), unless their jurisdiction is redistricted or there's some other large shift in the beliefs of their voter base. Often, you'll find favor with a strict partisan as long as you're on the same side as them, but might not get the time of day if you're on the opposing team. A partisan might take the time to read through and pass on the policy proposal if they agree with it, but might relegate it to the scrap pile if they disagree with it, or if it would harm their standing with their party. One of the major benefits of partisans, provided you're on the same side, is that they're rather effective in legislation, voting with the party a large percentage of the time. However, if you're on the opposite team, you might just have to wait it out until there's a chance to elect someone else.

Of course, each of the three models above are caricatures, and most representatives would fall under some combination of the three categories. Indeed, there's another often used category called a politico, which represents a mashup of the delegate and trustee categories. Additionally, candidates might change their framework depending on what their legislative jurisdiction looks like, as well as how it changes over time through changes in voter preferences and redistricting. However, many candidates lean towards one of the three, and fully understanding where your representative stands can better inform your decision of whether to vote for them in the future. It's also important to take into account how each type of candidate works at the national level. If you tend to be more partisan yourself, you might gravitate towards a partisan candidate who is less likely to listen to their constituents but more likely to vote along party lines in congress. Or, if your political ideology is a minority in the congressional district you live in, you might be more tempted to vote for a delegate or a trustee, as they might be more likely to either listen to your concerns or vote more independently on legislation. While it's important to recognize which candidates match up with your policy goals, it's also important to notice how candidates will represent those goals once they actually take office, and if those goals have the potential to change in the future.

While there are ways of determining whether a congressperson is more or less likely to listen to constituent concerns, there's no guarantee that this will actually result in a favored bill becoming a law. As mentioned in the aforementioned Schoolhouse Rock!^{TM} ditty, actually getting through the process from bill to law is *incredibly* difficult. To put this into perspective, at the time of writing this, in the 117th Congress (a congress that theoretically has a Democratic trifecta, although the Senate is technically a tie with Vice President Kamala Harris as the tiebreaker), 506 laws have been passed. During that same time period, 14,386 bills have been proposed. So, even with a theoretical Democratic Trifecta, only 3.5% of proposed bills actually made it into law. This is partly due to the bipartisanship necessary in order for bills to pass the final hurdle, but also due to the sheer legislative marathon that bills need to traverse in order to make it to the president's desk. While there are many different fantastic explanations of this process, I'll do my best to summarize the official House of Representatives' explanation of how a bill becomes a law here.

1. A law is first conceived as a humble idea in the mind of a private citizen, a representative, or a lobbyist. Probably a lobbyist.
2. A representative chooses to sponsor the bill, pledging their support for it throughout the process.
3. Depending on the contents of the bill, it is assigned to a particular committee, headed by a member of the party in control of the House or Senate, depending on what part of Congress the bill originates in. This is where most bills go to die, particularly if the committee head is a member of the opposite party of the bill's political leanings.
4. Once the bill passes though the committee, it's debated on the floor of Congress. Amendments might be added, or entire parts of the bill might be struck from the proposal.
5. The cycle repeats in the other chamber of Congress and, if the bill advances from its second committee, it is passed on to the floor of the other chamber for more debate and is probably amended again.
6. If the bill has survived this gauntlet of amendments, any discrepancies between the House and Senate's version of the bill are ironed out by a committee of House and Senate members before returning to each chamber to be voted on again.
7. If the revised bill passes through both chambers one last time, it advances to the president's desk. At this point, the president has three options. They can either sign it into law, veto it outright, or stall for 10 days, upon which a pocket veto occurs. A pocket veto is basically the presidential equivalent of procrastinating doing a task until it goes away. If the president vetoes the bill,

this decision can be overruled and the bill can become a law via a two-thirds vote in the House and the Senate. Pocket vetoes can be overruled by a two-thirds vote in the Senate, unless Congress has adjourned during this 10-day period, at which time the bill has to restart the process from the beginning. [61]

As you can see, it's an incredibly long and difficult process for a bill to become a law, and the different branches of Congress can perform different actions in order to make this process easier or harder. One of the most commonly used mechanisms of doing so is one you've probably heard of before: the filibuster. The filibuster is a process by which one member of the Senate alone can stall unwanted legislation, and it can only be broken if a large majority of senators (most recently 60/100, but the exact number can be changed) vote to end it. But what you might not have heard before is that the filibuster itself isn't mentioned in the Constitution. Indeed, it didn't even become part of the Senate until the 1850s,[62] and only serves as one tenet of the Senate rules, which can be (and often are) altered at the beginning of each Senate term. Early filibuster usage was to delay the ratification of the Treaty of Versailles, but more recently it has gained a track record for delaying civil rights legislations, including anti-lynching bills in the 1960s.[63] While the reasons for filibustering have remained similar over time, the method itself has changed considerably. Historically, the vast majority of filibusters have consisted of a speaker talking on the Senate floor for hours on end to delay legislation, at least until the Senate reaches a 60 vote cloture, which automatically ends that talking filibuster. The unfortunate record for the longest talking filibuster goes to Strom Thurmond, who filibustered the Civil Rights Act of 1957 for a total of 24 hours and 18 minutes. It should also be noted that other opponents of the Civil Rights Act worked together to filibuster the act for 57 days until it was finally passed.[64] However, the filibuster itself looks slightly different today. While the 60 vote majority to achieve cloture remains, as of 2022 senators don't need to even speak on the floor of the Senate in order to keep a filibuster alive. Rather, bills that don't immediately receive 60 votes in the Senate are considered to be filibustered, and are often pronounced dead soon after.

The filibuster itself represents something of a game of political chicken. If one party with enough of a majority were to remove the filibuster, they could pass an incredibly strong legislative agenda, shaping the country in their desired image. However, this could come back to bite them in the future. If the opposing party were to come into power, they would have a similar lack of opposition in passing their policy priorities. At the moment, both parties seem content with the safer option, making bills more difficult to pass, but also providing damage control against the party in power's whims. Unfortunately, this tool can also handcuff the government of the United States, decreasing its efficiency and increasing gridlock. In order to balance the pros and cons of this system, there are some other options that could balance requiring bipartisan support for bills while also making bills easier to pass.

One option, of course, is removing the filibuster entirely, which would lead to rapidly increasing legislative success on both sides of the aisle, while the actual bills passed would tend to be more partisan. Another solution would be to return to the filibuster rules of the 1970s, where a senator must be speaking at all times in order to keep the filibuster going. This would reduce the chances of a Filibuster completely derailing legislation, but could also take up valuable time that could be spent passing other laws. Additionally, the Senate could require a number of opposing senators (let's say, 40, to mirror the 60 votes required to break cloture and end a filibuster) to remain in the Senate at all times in order to maintain a filibuster. Once less than 40 senators are in the Senate chamber, cloture would be considered reached, the filibuster would end, and legislation could continue with a majority vote. Finally, the number of senators required for cloture could be changed from 60 to 55 to even 51, requiring some semblance of bipartisan support without setting the bar too high. A similar solution would be requiring a certain number of senators from each party to vote for a bill to ensure its safe passage.

Needless to say, if one hopes for a more successful and productive Congress, there are multiple steps that the Senate can take almost immediately that would only require a majority vote to change Senate rules.

Outside of the filibuster, one major feature of the Senate that distinguishes it from the House of Representatives is how its members are elected. Rather than giving states representatives based on population like the House does, each of the United States is allocated two senators regardless of population. Accordingly, California's population of 40 million receives just as many votes in the Senate as Wyoming's 600,000. The reasons for this start with the aforementioned Constitutional Convention. During the convention (which is always, for some reason, stressed as being held during an uncharacteristically hot summer, which has always struck me as odd. I'm sure it was hot, but I'm sure that the delegates saw it as a pretty characteristically hot summer, due to them being used to the lack of air conditioning) held in 1787, the uncharacteristically hot delegates were unable to reach a satisfying agreement concerning exactly how our Legislative branch would function. Larger states found themselves in favor of proportional representation, as this system would allow them more future delegates to Congress than the smaller states, and would more closely represent the one person, one vote ideal upon which democracy was based. The less populous states didn't like this deal very much, and the measure was unable to pass. These smaller states hoped for some form of state based representation, which would reject the principle of one person one vote, but would allow smaller states to have the same amount of weight as larger ones in the legislature. The measure even threatened the convention itself, so long did the disagreement persist. Neither side was willing to potentially give up power to the other, but most also recognized the benefits of having some kind of Legislative branch to counter the Executive and Judicial branches. After much arguing, Roger Sherman and Oliver Ellsworth of Connecticut came up with a compromise. A Great Compromise, it might even be said. This Great Compromise, drawing from the British government in addition to different state constitutions, proposed a bicameral (two branch) legislature. The House of Representatives would be based on population, while the Senate would allocate two senators to each state.[65] Even still, the Great Compromise succeeded by just one vote. While the compromise held the country together during a time that the Constitution could have been torn asunder and rewritten, it was one of the first steps away from the democratic ideals the country was based on, and towards something else entirely.

Due to this Great Compromise, the Senate and the House of Representatives function a little bit differently, and require different types of candidates. Representatives, on one hand, serve relatively small populations of relatively small sections of a state (except for those of Alaska, Wyoming, Montana, North Dakota, South Dakota, Vermont, and Delaware, who serve an entire state due to their state's small population size). This means that each hopeful Representative must appeal to a relatively small slice of America, one that is more homogeneous than the national or state average, and one that can easily be traversed in a short period of time. Accordingly, the politics of representatives can be as variable as the constituencies they hope to represent, resulting in a more politically heterogeneous House of Representatives. The House therefore has an incredibly wide variety of political views represented within it, as the full spectrum of political ideologies are represented by America's 435 districts. As a result of the small size of districts, every single Representative faces a re-election battle every two years, rather than senators, who face re-election every six. The House of Representatives is constantly changing, and is therefore incredibly reactive to the news of the day. A shift in the country's political mood can cause huge ripple effects throughout the House of Representatives, as members whose politics don't align with these changes can lose their seats almost as quickly as they won them. Additionally, backlash against a newly-elected president often causes their party to lose control of the House in the two years after the presidential election, as only two presidents in the past 90 years have ever won seats in the midterm elections that occur two years after winning an election. These two presidents, Franklin Delano Roosevelt in 1934 and George W. Bush in 2002, benefitted from two periods of massive voter consolidation around their party after the success of the New Deal and after the terrorist attacks of September 11, 2001.[66]

The Senate, however, remains just a bit more stable. Instead of every two years, senators are elected every six years in a staggered order. Every two years, one-third of all senators face a re-election campaign. Senators also often have to cover a lot more territory, as they're expected to represent a whole state, rather than simply a small chunk of one. While representatives are able to often win their election by appealing to the changing sensibilities of their constituents, senators have a different mountain to climb to win election and re-election. Senators have to represent entire states, often composed of multiple different larger cities, rings of suburbs surrounding the cities, and large swaths of rural areas. Each level of population represents citizens with differing political ideologies, differing demographics, and differing levels of political engagement. In order to succeed, senators must not only be savvy at discerning the policy preferences of a large chunk of America, but they must also be master persuaders, convincing the undecided to not just vote, but to vote for them. Granted, senators have a little bit more time to do this, as their six year terms allow them more time to understand the sensibilities of their voters. In order to secure the office in the first place, however, senators must be incredibly good politicians that are able to appeal to the majority of a state's population of voters. Not an easy task. You'll often find that senators are more moderate than their Representative counterparts, and less reactive to the news of the day. As they're elected every six years, the news occurring multiple years before their re-election has little to no effect on their election prospects. Rather than focusing on the news of the day, successful senators pay attention to long term shifts in voter preferences, those that can be proved by years of data and trends. Just as senators are less reactive to events occurring at the moment, the makeup of the Senate is similarly less reactive to these events. If only one third of senators are elected every two years, the majority of senators are completely immune to the negative effects that House members are subject to after the election of a president. Often, senators are able to play this to their advantage, holding their Senate seats for somewhat longer periods of time.

On this subject, at the beginning of the 117th Congress, the average senator had served for 11 years (so far), while the average Congressperson had served for nine years.[67] Additionally, the median senator and Congressperson were 63 and 58 years old,[68] respectively, while the median age in America is a comparatively youthful 38.[69] While at least some of this can be explained by the age requirements of the House and Senate (25 and 30, respectively), it's odd that the average age of our government officials is significantly higher than that of its citizens. While there might be seemingly legitimate reasons for this, as it's possible that voters believe older candidates to be more qualified to hold public office, it's particularly worrying to recognize how much older congresspeople are than the constituents they represent. While the average service time for senators and representatives falls somewhere around 10 years, this doesn't necessarily tell the whole story of why our congresspeople are so much older on average. To find out why, it's also important to look at how some senators and representatives can stay in office for so long.

When elections occur nationally, there is a relatively consistent turnover between Democrats and Republicans. Over the past 40 years, there have been eight different presidents in office, four Democrats and four Republicans. Out of those 40 years, both parties have found similar amounts of success in the oval office, with both parties winning a total of six terms in office. This means that during this 40 year period, every president has won re-election somewhere between 50% and 66% of the time, depending on whether they're a Republican or Democrat, respectively.[70] However, in the same 40 years, members of the House of Representatives achieved re-election about 90% of the time, while members of the Senate won re-election about 85% of the time.

There are a number of reasons for this range in percentages. First and foremost, the Presidential election is a national one, and the country as a whole is much more ideologically balanced than the majority of states and representative districts. Presidential elections are generally close calls, and even if a candidate wins the vast majority of electors, the popular vote rarely is won by more than a margin of 10%. However, individual states, and especially legislative districts, can be less ideologically balanced, leading to one party controlling the area for a longer period of time, as well as heavy advantages for their incumbents seeking re-election.

The longer an individual is in office, the more money they can raise from donors and from the party. But, there's one feature that the Presidency has that congressional positions don't that contributes to its higher rate of party turnover: the term limit. You see, term limits weren't actually established for the president until the 22nd amendment was passed in 1951.[71] Prior to that, the vast majority of presidents had only served up to two terms (I'm looking at you, FDR) out of a historical precedent set by George Washington, a sort of unwritten rule of the presidency if you will. No such precedent has ever been set for members of the House of Representatives and the Senate, leading to these congresspeople enjoying long, financially fulfilling careers on Capitol Hill. These long careers are a double-edged sword. Enjoying a long career in Congress can lead to a high level of legislative proficiency, and long careers can make old timers more effective than rookies learning the ropes. However, these long careers can also lead to stagnancy, as representatives learn that they can keep their offices relatively easily provided they sustain basic constituent services and legislate similarly enough to their constituents' preferences. Even if a newer, younger candidate would eventually become a better representative or senator than the incumbent, it's incredibly hard to actually unseat an incumbent. One reason for this is one mentioned earlier in this book: the concept of name recognition. People often find confidence in safety, and particularly if a voter doesn't have the time to research each candidate running, they're very likely to vote for the name that they know, who is likely to be the incumbent. Provided the incumbent isn't screwing up too badly, voters can often go with the more comfortable choice. Additionally, the incumbent has a proven history of winning general elections, meaning that even well-informed voters are more likely to select an incumbent in the primaries, as they're generally thought to be the best option against the opposition, considering they've won before.

Term limits are one possible way to protect against the incumbent advantage, periodically shaking up congressional and Senate races by allowing other candidates to compete. If an incumbent is guaranteed to not be able to run in the next election, it opens up the seat to other potential challengers, resulting in much more competitive primaries and (theoretically) better candidates. Then, if the seasoned veteran can't run for their seat, it forces them to attempt to run for another elected position if they want to stay in politics, potentially shaking up that race as well. Currently, 15 states have term limits for their state legislatures, but no limits are in place at the federal level outside of the presidency. It's important to note that term limits aren't perfect solutions. Presidents in their second term can be subject to *lame duck* presidencies, in which they pursue less legislative and policy changes due to the fact that they don't need to run for election anymore. Because of this, it's important to ensure that all term limit propositions should consider the tradeoff of possible lame duck terms in lieu of the complacency that can come from a lack of term limits.

The importance of the Legislative branch of government can't be overstated, but this branch of government isn't without its pros and cons. While the ingenuity of the Great Compromise kept the Constitution alive in one of its darker moments, its concessions allowed Congress to become less representative of people and more representative of states as a whole. The lack of term limits can also cause representatives to become complacent the longer they remain in office, or potentially become better legislators, provided they have the stamina and willpower to continue fighting for their constituents. The topic of the length of one's tenure in government will be considered further in the next chapter, as we explore the one branch of government whose members are elected for life: the Judicial branch.

Chapter 7: The Judicial Branch

The founding and original location of the highest court of the Judicial branch, the Supreme Court, allows us a brief glimpse into an often forgotten truth of the first few decades of the United States: the polished marble and sandstone adorning the current Capitol in Washington, D.C. is a more recent invention, and some of the most important decisions made regarding our early government occurred in borrowed space. For example, the first ever meeting of the Supreme Court took place in the Merchants Exchange building in New York City (the Capital at the time), and the Supreme Court itself didn't have a permanent home until 1935, when it finally settled into its current location in Washington, D.C.[72] Even though the Judicial branch of the U.S. Government is unique among the three branches for not occupying the same space for the majority of its tenure, its effect on the political landscape throughout history is unquestionable.

To create the Judicial branch, the Constitution established a Supreme Court, with judges nominated by the president and confirmed by Congress. Additionally, it said that Congress has the power to establish lower courts below the Supreme Court, and that justices were to serve for life during "good behavior."[72] However, the Supreme Court that we have today is pretty far from the one that was established by the Constitution in 1788. For starters, the original Supreme Court was made up of six total justices, with a Chief Justice leading the five other Associate Justices. This composition only lasted a short period of time, with the court contracting to five total justices in 1801, expanding back to six justices soon after, and further expanding to seven justices in 1807. In 1837, the court expanded once more to nine justices, another time to 10 during the Civil War, all the way back down to seven after the War, until an 1869 Judiciary Act reset the number to nine judges, where it stands to this day (although FDR attempted to change that during his administration, proposing an addition of up to six new justices, but his plan failed and the court remained at 9).[73] I mention this incredibly long laundry list of changes not to bore or confuse you, though it almost certainly did both, but to simply illustrate how the court has changed over time, and that the same arguments existing today regarding the number of Supreme Court justices aren't exactly new.

This is particularly important since theoretically, the members of the Supreme Court should technically be among the most powerful, if not *the* most powerful, members of the United States Government, even rivaling the president in their power over time. While presidents are able to wield a very significant microphone, using the bully pulpit to try to force legislation over the line, there's little that they can actually do to force a bill through Congress if Congress doesn't want to pass the bill. They have unilateral power to prevent laws from passing, but can be overridden by a united Congress and only serve for eight years at the most, limiting their power over time. A rather competent senator or member of the House of Representatives can enjoy a long period of time in office, but they are still beholden to their voters, and are just one member in an incredibly large legislative body. When it comes down to it, there's only so much one representative or senator can do. Supreme Court justices, on the other hand, are meant to be much less swayed by the general American public. While they're originally appointed by a president and confirmed by Congress, they're pretty much left to freely roam upon being sworn into office, especially due to the fact that they hold their position in office for the rest of their lives. Sure, Supreme Court justices can be removed from office if they violate their "good behavior" clause, but this has only ever happened once in the history of the United States, when Justice Samuel Chase was impeached by the House of Representatives. He subsequently was acquitted by the Senate, and kept his job.[74] Additionally, the number of justices alone contributes to the power that they have. While there are significantly more Supreme Court justices than presidents, they also don't have to deal with the legislative bureaucracy of attempting to make decisions through the long and painstaking processes of Congress. This isn't to say that Supreme Court decisions are passed out like hotcakes, but the ability to quickly determine the meaning of a passed law, or strike it down entirely with a simple majority of five, is an incredibly effective power indeed. A good analogy might be that of a car. If Congress represents the gear shift, driving the car forwards or pushing it backwards, and the president acts as the steering wheel, determining exactly where the legislation will go and how, the Supreme Court acts as the brakes. If the brakes are applied, no matter how hard you push the gas pedal or how hard you turn the steering wheel, you know for sure that the car is going nowhere. You could even make the argument that the Supreme Court has power over the gear shift as well, throwing the car into reverse if they deem it necessary. If a car has brakes that can't be removed from office, aren't accountable to voters, and can be applied at any time, it's going to be incredibly hard for that car to go forward unless the brakes are disengaged.

Fortunately, the brakes have, at least until recently, a relatively proven track record of knowing when the car should go, and when the car should stop. Historically, the Supreme Court has enjoyed a significantly higher approval rating when compared to the other branches of government,[75] at least until the current day (we'll get to that in a moment). One of the major reasons behind this is the concept that Supreme Court justices tend to have a record for being nonpartisan actors. Justices don't run for office under any particular political party, and it's their legal interpretation of the Constitution that is called "liberal" or "conservative," rather than any political ideology itself. They don't represent political parties, they don't endorse candidates, and they attempt to avoid weighing in on any political decisions currently being made that aren't being directly considered by their court. Most of the time, at least. There's a rather major reason why Supreme Court justices try their absolute hardest to appear nonpartisan, and it's one that occurs due to a certain omission from their list of duties. This omission alone can drastically reduce the aforementioned power of the Supreme Court, particularly if they lose the trust of the people who put them in their positions. Simply put, the Supreme Court has no way to actually enforce the rulings that they make. The Supreme Court can make as many rulings as it wishes to, but it relies on the Executive branch, and indirectly the Legislative branch, to enforce their rulings if they hope to have any power whatsoever. Without the power of the Executive branch to back them up, the Supreme Court is reduced to little more than a bunch of Ivy league law degrees in fancy robes yelling at clouds. Of course, presidents who openly defy Supreme Court decisions open the door to impeachment and conviction, however, given the track record of zero presidential convictions in almost 250 years it's more than a little surprising that more overzealous heads of state haven't taken their chances.

To see what would happen if this played out, let's return closer to the present day and consider the 2022 Supreme Court ruling overturning Roe v. Wade, removing the constitutional right to abortion. In the wake of this, the court itself experienced a fair amount of backlash in public opinion, dropping their approval rating from 40% to 25% in two years, by far its lowest approval rating in the past half-decade.[76] In theory, President Joe Biden and governors in states with abortion bans in effect could take the position that the court's ruling is illegitimate, and instruct its police departments to stop enforcing any abortion ban. Would the President or governor face backlash from voters, as well as numerous legal challenges and impeachment threats for refusing to accept the legitimacy of a Supreme Court ruling? Possibly. Would the Supreme Court be able to do anything to stop the state or national Executive branch from doing so? No, not really.

There's a little bit of precedence for this. In 1832, the Supreme Court ruled that Andrew Jackson couldn't forcibly remove Native Americans from their birthplaces, basing their decision on Georgia's already existing state law that gave Native Americans rights to the land they lived on. Jackson allegedly remarked that "John Marshall (the Chief Justice at the time) has made his decision, now let him enforce it,"[77] the presidential equivalent of "nah, nah, na boo boo, you can't catch me." Following his remark, he continued establishing what later came to be known as the Trail of Tears, killing over 3,000 Native Americanson only the first of many forced marches to Oklahoma in one of the most egregious examples of American cruelty to date.[78] Enforce it Marshall couldn't, and the only retribution Jackson could have faced was a political one, which didn't really matter as his second term in office was ending soon anyway.

Due to the general lack of means of enforcement, the Supreme Court has generally benefited from being as balanced as possible, giving the appearance of nonpartisanship whenever it can in order to maintain legitimacy among the other branches of government and among the American people. While Supreme Court justices often hold their specific political views close to their chest, their judicial ideologies can be relatively easily discerned through the decisions they make, as well as their judicial reasoning for making these decisions. Legal precedent often takes center stage in these explanations, as previous similar cases are an important guideline for future decisions. However, those cases where there isn't any clear precedent, as well as Justices' Senate hearings, when they are bombarded with questions regarding their legal philosophy, provide us with a good look into how they make decisions and how these decisions change over time. For a clearer demonstration, here is a glimpse into how the Supreme Court has shifted ideologically over time, both when new justices are added and when the political landscape changes:

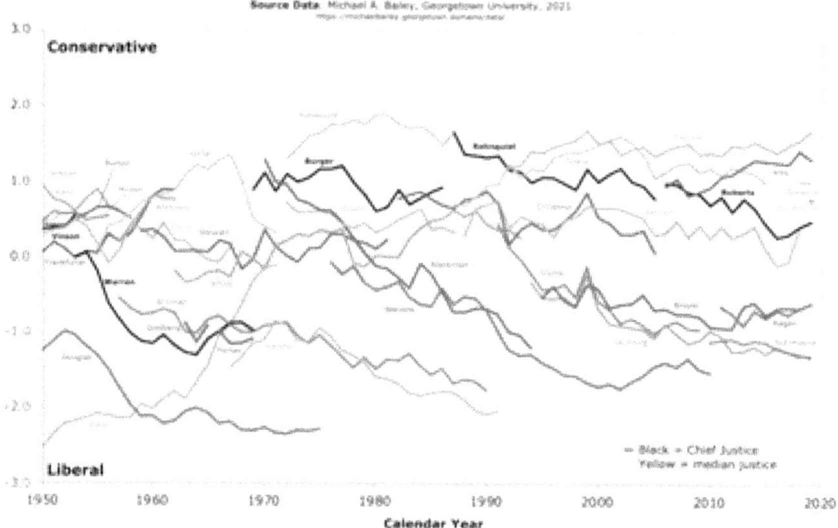

Wikimedia Commons[79]

This chart, which is only slightly less confusing and illegible than it appears, tracks the judicial philosophy of the Supreme Court justices from 1950 until 2020. For our purposes, let's stick with recent memory, and look only at the justices who have served after 2010. As we can see, the justices who served longest between 2010 and 2020 have moved in rather different directions in this time period. Since 2010, Justices Kagan, Alito, and Thomas have tended to grow more conservative, while Sotomayor, Ginsburg, and especially Chief Justice John Roberts have grown more liberal. While Kavanaugh and Gorsuch haven't been in office long enough at this point to truly get a read of their movement over time, the recent six-three overturning of Roe v. Wade indicates that they are likely to maintain their conservatism to some degree. However, there are two justices that I would like to focus on in particular, Chief Justice John Roberts and Brett Kavanaugh. Both justices were appointed by Republican presidents, and would be expected to have relatively conservative judicial ideologies. If the Supreme Court, which as I am writing this is dominated six-three by conservative ideology, does indeed wish to appear nonpartisan, one would expect some of the conservative justices to take a slight turn towards the liberal ideology. While I don't think anyone expects Kavanaugh or Roberts to fully take on a liberal judicial ideology, it wouldn't be out of the realm of possibility for the aforementioned Justices to occasionally vote in favor of a more liberal-leaning ruling, or at least write a less strict opinion on a conservative-leaning ruling. While it appears that Justice John Roberts might have begun to follow this trend from 2005 through about 2015, he appears to have taken a turn back towards the right, and the aforementioned Roe v. Wade decision indicates that Kavanaugh and Gorsuch, and therefore the Supreme Court as a whole, might be looking to follow suit. As could probably be expected, the population of the United States is beginning to feel this partisan shift, indicated by the drastic reduction of the Supreme Court's approval rating from 40% all the way down to 25%. Make no mistake, these next few years will be an interesting test to see exactly how far the Supreme Court's control can stretch. If the conservative wing of the Supreme Court can realign to present a less partisan wing, then it's possible that the Supreme Court can regain some sense of credibility. However, if they continue to remain an overly conservative court, then it's hard to not see some version of court reform in the near future as progressives and progressive-leaning moderates begin to feel disenfranchised.

The idea of Supreme Court reform is a politically fraught one. Due to the control that Congress is afforded over reforming the Supreme Court, doing so improperly (and even doing so properly) can lead to accusations of politicizing the court or using the court to their political advantage, which can impact the reputations of both Congress and the Supreme Court itself. So, what exactly would Supreme Court reform look like? Let's start from the most commonly occurring or more obvious forms, then move on to the more esoteric.

1. **Packing it up**

The most obvious and commonly occurring concept that comes to mind is often known as *court packing*, or adding members to the Supreme Court. Doing so ideally reduces any current imbalances of the court, and reforms it into an ideologically balanced institution. Of course, when done incorrectly, it can lead to an even larger partisan imbalance. This action is generally preferable to shrinking the size of the court, as I can imagine it's a particularly difficult (not to mention possibly Unconstitutional) job to tell a Supreme Court justice that they've been axed to make the court more ideologically balanced.

Pros: The size of the court has been expanded and contracted several times throughout the history of the United States, and the precedence is there. Congress has the constitutional power to do so.

Cons: Expanding or contracting the size of the Supreme Court is incredibly hard to do without political backlash. Even if the court is already unbalanced, adding members who are sympathetic to your own party's interests tends to rile up your political opponents. Additionally, setting the precedent of court packing makes it that much easier for your opponent to do the same once they enter office, leading to a possible slippery slope of expansion and contraction to suit political needs.

2. **Imposing a Code of Ethics**

Many of the lower courts, including all federal justices, are required to abide by a code of ethics, which requires judges to (paraphrased): be faithful to the law, maintain competence in it, maintain order and decorum, avoid partisanship, and many others. If federal judges don't follow this code of ethics, it can be used against them in a future impeachment trial. Actually, as this book was in the process of being published, the Supreme Court decided to impose a Code of Ethics on themselves. Time will tell if it will prove to be successful, or if it will need to be adapted to be more effective.

Pros: As federal judges and those in the lower courts are already bound by a code of ethics, it wouldn't be too difficult to expand these codes to the Supreme Court. Additionally, around 72% of Americans would favor a code of ethics being implemented,[82] and it therefore would be a rather bipartisan plan. As Supreme Court justices have never been successfully removed from office, there's a certain sense of invincibility surrounding the position, and providing the possibility of censure could incentivize good behavior.

Cons: While a code of ethics would certainly help, there's no guarantee that it could actually be enforced properly, or that Congress would actually want to enforce it. The track record of Congress actually removing public officials from office is incredibly poor, and it's possible that this solution could just be a slap on the wrist rather than actually providing legitimate repercussions. It would also do very little to correct any partisan leans in the Court in the way that other types of reform could.

3.   **Term limits**

Personally, I believe that enacting term limits for Supreme Court justices is one of the most likely options for court reform. Polls indicate that around 67% of Americans would currently support it,[80] and it would ensure that Supreme Court justices are closer to their peak mentally. Additionally, it would disincentivize the current practice of appointing the youngest possible qualified candidate in hopes that they will stay on the bench longer. There would also likely be less negative backlash from the opposite party, as term limits don't obviously benefit either party in the long run.

Pros: It wouldn't have the immediate backlash of packing the courts, and is a measure that a majority of Americans currently support. It would incentivize appointing the most qualified, effective candidates, and would ensure that justices are mentally and physically healthy enough to preside well.

Cons: The Constitution has established that Supreme Court justices should rule for life, and changing that would require a constitutional amendment, an incredibly difficult process to succeed at. Additionally, Supreme Court justices are given lifetime appointments to supposedly be above the politics of the day, looking more at the climate of an era. Shortening the amount of time they're in office might cause them to be more nearsighted in their rulings, particularly if their term is coming to a close.

4. **A more creative style of reform**

There's more than one way to change the size of the court, and sometimes thinking outside of the box might just be the best option. There's been a variety of ways to overhaul how the court works, but one that comes to mind is current Secretary of Transportation Pete Buttigieg's plan to reform the Supreme Court that he rolled out during the 2020 presidential election primaries.[81] His plan involved changing the court to automatically include 15 justices: five liberal, five conservative, and five apolitical, who have been chosen by the first 10. Alternate plans could have some justices occupying one of several partisan positions appointed by a president of their political party whenever a vacancy occurs, while the other "swing" justices can be appointed by whoever is president when a vacancy occurs. This plan, and others like it, would do better to avoid the explicit partisan leanings of the current court, while possibly avoiding the ire of political opponents who would be turned off by a simple addition or deletion of justices.

Pros: In contrast to court packing, this solution would ensure that the Supreme Court stays relatively balanced over a long period of time. It would also be harder to attack this solution as being strictly a partisan ploy, as it would give each party an equal chance to control the Court.

Cons: There isn't much precedent in the Constitution to reform the Court in this way, indicating that an amendment would be necessary to actually pass it. It would openly admit that Supreme Court justices are indeed partisan, as many of the justices would hold an explicitly partisan office, something that the Supreme Court has attempted to deny since its creation.

While most Americans support Supreme Court reform to some degree, there are certainly some rather large obstacles standing in the way, as the majority of solutions would require a constitutional amendment. However, there's certainly a roadmap to reform, provided that enough Americans put their opinions behind one particular solution to push it across the finish line.

But how do people form opinions in the first place? How do we determine which ones to fight for in the political sphere? What role do news organizations themselves play in molding and shaping the opinions of citizens? The news we consume and the media networks that shovel it to our waiting maws play a rather large role in the types of policies and solutions we prefer, and the nuances (and dangers) of this will be discussed at length in the next section.

Chapter 8: News and the Media

The news is everywhere. There's local news stations, print and online newspapers, cable news, podcasts, radio shows, Instagram accounts, Facebook feeds, books (hello!), Twitter threads, blogs, and so much more, not to mention simply talking to friends and family. We're absolutely surrounded by news sources, seemingly all of the time now. Unfortunately, the veracity of these news sources is incredibly variable. Sure, there's the occasional hidden gem news organization that produces nonpartisan, "just the facts" coverage, but there are so many others that produce spin, bias, or even just downright lies. Even the "good" ones aren't perfect. How on earth are we supposed to sift through the mountain of rubbish in order to find any semblance of truth? How do we know the difference between what is real, and what's an incredibly well-fabricated lie? How can we tell if even the best news sources are telling the objective truth, or just one particular version of it? If we hope to determine which news sources are better than others, then our journey starts with determining what exactly the "truth" we're seeking is. Of course, this is an incredibly difficult endeavor. I'm sure that despite our best efforts, this chapter will fall far short in determining what some exact "truths" even are. No matter how clearly we distill the "truth," it's likely that there will still be some disagreements, and that's okay. Disagreements are a sign of a healthy democracy, as long as those disagreements are based on similar facts, or at least a search for common truths. Sometimes, things that seem true to some might be completely rejected by others, due to differences in upbringing and lived experience. This is a natural consequence of the diversities and nuances of experience that make life interesting. Where we begin to run into the most trouble, however, is when these "facts" are purposefully twisted and altered in order to fit a particular political agenda, rather than building a political agenda around certain truths and the beliefs that spring from them.

Unfortunately, America seems to be entering a period of time where the former is occurring, rather than the latter. The largest news corporations are pursuing political and financial advantages, rather than searching for an objective truth. In order to avoid America being ripped in two, the motivations of political media need to change from those of personal gain to those of uncovering the truth, regardless of possible political or financial gain. Achieving this is no easy task, however, and it requires the media on both sides sacrificing potential gains in exchange for a greater good. If only. However, this isn't necessarily impossible. The news environment of today is a different one than 300 years ago, or even 100 years ago, with different motivations and different reward structures. Possibly, in order to improve the news of the future, it is important to first look at the past.

The form and function of news media has changed dramatically since its inception. The first conceptions of "news" were incredibly, incredibly slow. Like, as far as word of mouth can travel slow. In fact, some of the earliest forms of news were just that: tidbits of information passed around by word of mouth. As one could imagine, this breaking news went only as quickly as a human could run, or shout. In fact, one of the earlier instances of breaking news revolves around a Greek messenger who, upon hearing about a Greek victory over invading Persia, ran over 25 miles from Marathon to Athens to spread the good news. Upon delivering his message, he collapsed and died. For his good early journalism skills (as well as his running ability), his journey from the city of Marathon became the namesake of a particular 26.2 mile running competition that's been part of every single modern Olympic games.[83] Not bad for an early journalist. As time has passed, several inventions have made the dissemination of news not only easier, but also exponentially faster. One of the first forms of journalism was the invention of the job of the Town Crier. Upon receiving an important announcement (often directly from the King or Queen themselves), the town crier would stand in the middle of the town square, repeat the announcement for all to hear, and then conclude with a "God Save the King/Queen," before posting the written declaration on the door of the town's inn.[84]

During the time of the town crier, dissemination of news was from the top down, from the most powerful to the least. Kings and Queens had almost ultimate control over the content of the news, and could therefore use this to their advantage, prioritizing self-enhancing news while neglecting to release news that could put themselves in a bad light. This top-down system of news put everyday people at an incredible disadvantage. Not only did commoners have no control over the news whatsoever, but it was incredibly difficult to dispute any possible discrepancies due to a lack of education, or even lack of knowledge about the goings-on of the kingdom. If the queen tells you that an army is mobilizing past the western mountain range, and that you need to provide your most fit son for battle, who are you to believe differently? Are you really going to go check and risk the ire of the crown? That's a good way to get thrown in the stocks. Additionally, the vast majority of individuals couldn't read or write at this time, so they couldn't create pamphlets or newsletters or early newspapers of their own. If they wished to share their own news, they had to do so using word of mouth. If any of you have ever played the game telephone, you likely know exactly how problematic this can be. Messages can easily become distorted the more they're passed on, especially if it's a juicy piece of gossip. Unfortunately, this works both ways, and if royalty can tell commoners anything they want about themselves, and only tell them good things, it's incredibly easy for royalty to take on a God-like, super powerful, invincible status. Of course, this isn't exactly ideal for the members of a feudal system in which the vast majority weren't educated, owned no land for themselves, and were largely only fed by portions of the land they worked for someone else.[85]

Now we can identify the first problem with news media, one that persists over time: who controls the news? While the first forms of news were controlled directly by the ruler of the land, other inventions allowed others to take more control over the process itself. Arguably the most impactful invention for journalism (and honestly, arguably the most impactful invention of all time) was Gutenberg's printing press, invented in Germany in 1429. Not only did the printing press allow books to be produced much quicker and cheaper, it also increased their accessibility. With this increase in accessibility also came an interest in learning to read and write, activities usually only reserved for the wealthy in previous years. Literacy skyrocketed, and with it came a need to revolutionize how news spread. By the 1600s, printers in Europe and Japan had begun to publish the most rudimentary newspapers, pamphlets often reporting a single topical event. However, as printing became easier, printers found that they could publish more events in the same pamphlet at the same time, and the modern newspaper was born. With this creation came the next iteration of our current problem: who actually owns the means of disseminating news, and who is able to control it? The beginning of the modern newspaper also started an ink-stained revolution—the establishment of independent publishing companies. Now, those publishing the newspaper (rather than the individual in power) began to have control over what news was published, how it was published, and what would be left out. As could be expected, this often didn't quite sit well with rulers, who had, until recently, held a monopoly on this particular method of informing the public. In America's 13 colonies, this proved to be a problem for early newspapers, particularly those who were against British rule. Indeed, the first newspaper ever published in the colonies was silenced by the governor of the colony after just its first issue. Newspapers became one of the most important battle grounds during the American Revolution (outside of, you know, *the* battle ground), building support for the Revolution while simultaneously risking execution for treason against the British Government.[86] With this as a backdrop, it makes sense that after the American Revolution concluded with the former colonies on top, the very first amendment to the Constitution was the establishment of a free press.

While the first question regarding the press has been answered, indicating that the press is beholden to the people reading it, rather than the government itself, another question facing journalism sprung forth. Now, publishers had to determine what exactly to publish, as well as what standards they should hold themselves to. Newspapers, oddly enough, started off much more partisan than they are today. From their infancy to about the 1950s, they rarely sought middle ground, and often sought to report the news in a way that benefited their own political faction. It wasn't until the 1950's that newspapers began to shift more towards fact-based reporting. Apart from objectively more factual reporting, some evidence of this comes from the establishment of the Society of Professional Journalists' code of ethics, created in 1947 to establish regulations in reporting the news. These ethics include, among other things, taking responsibility for one's work, prioritizing accuracy over speed, providing context, identifying sources, giving voice to the voiceless, and labeling and separating commentary from fact-based journalism.[87] While newspapers today are certainly far from perfect, this code of conduct has helped shape the course of journalism from one of strict partisanship towards one that at least seeks truth, even if it doesn't always achieve it.

Another important question to consider is why exactly newspapers sought journalistic integrity in the first place. One rather obvious reason is that they were very much forced to. In 1949, reading the typeface on the wall and recognizing that such extreme partisanship in media was unsustainable, the Federal Communications Commision (FCC) passed the Fairness Doctrine, requiring news organizations to present the opinions from both sides if they were reporting on any political or otherwise non fact-based story. Additionally, individuals who felt they were being unfairly targeted were legally granted a right to publicly reply. This doctrine applied not only to the older news forms like newspapers, but also to the newer forms like radio and the ever-growing-in-popularity television. During these first decades of new media, the United States enjoyed a period of less severe partisanship. Media was legally required to report both sides, and the political parties themselves were overall closer to the center. After this time period, partisanship in congress has steadily increased to the levels we see today.[88]

While the gradual separation of each party into individual, rarely overlapping camps has undoubtedly played a role in the increase of partisanship in the news, it's likely that Ronald Reagan's 1987 repeal of the Fairness Doctrine likely played some role as well. Even though the Fairness Doctrine played a key role in reducing partisan bias in the media, opponents of the Doctrine claimed that it violated the first amendment, reducing the ability of journalists and publishers to publish their own opinion without it being diluted by the opposing side's viewpoint. While I personally would make the claim that being able to summarize an opponent's argument and counter it would actually increase the persuasiveness of one's own argument, this edition of the FCC didn't see it the same way, and decided to rule in favor of Reagan and strike down their previous guidelines. As a result, we've seen an increase in partisan media and increased partisanship in Congress and the general electorate. While it doesn't appear that any version of the Fairness Doctrine could or would be replaced anytime soon, I think you'd be hard pressed to find someone who believes that an increase in partisan negativity is necessarily a good thing, and if it isn't countered, it appears that the problem will only get worse. So, we find ourselves in a bit of a pickle. Our media environment is only becoming more partisan, yet it's almost impossible for either side to back down without putting themselves at risk of losing a competitive advantage in the media sphere. In order to figure out where to go from here, and how to solve the problem, it might be important to take a look at what individual issues are causing this partisanship, as well as what we can do to solve them.

At the lowest level, one of the main causes of partisanship in our news system (and one of the hardest to control) is the concept of bias. Strictly speaking, everyone has a bias, and everyone has a political one. No matter how down-the-middle a journalist's reporting seems to be, there will always be certain biases in terms of what they say, or often just as importantly, what they don't say. Realistically, avoiding all bias in our media environment is impossible, especially since not all biases are conscious. Short of putting each article through a giant panel of individuals who screen each word, said or left unsaid, for partisan slant, it's going to be completely impossible to eliminate bias entirely from journalism. Sure, if you're a journalist you might recognize your bias towards liberalism or conservatism, but you might not realize that the majority of your stories cover government spending, while only a few have been dedicated to civil rights legislation, for example. This problem is expanded at the editorial level, as they're able to control what the entire newspaper publishes, and what its entire circulation reads. If these biases are unconscious, no amount of trying will be able to fully solve the problem. However, one possible solution is actually making those biases clear from the very beginning. Sure, we know that Fox News is conservative and MSNBC is liberal, but the lean of other news sources (like local news and newspapers) is sometimes slightly harder to determine. If journalists had a way to list their biases prior to a publication, or if news organizations publicized the political preferences of their anchors and writers, it could possibly lead to more clarity on how their content could be biased, even if the biases aren't apparent at first.

While this idea may sound like it could work in theory, I can already see a major flaw. If the political preferences of media members are publicized, it could rather easily lead to more partisanship if individuals only choose to consume content from those they already agree with.

Actually, this concept in particular has been weighing rather heavily in my mind as I attempt to write this book. I'm personally progressive-minded, as you may or may not have been able to discern. I've wondered how many people would immediately stop reading the book if I made my political biases clear from the beginning. However, I do believe that the topics of this book could prove incredibly useful for progressives, conservatives, and everyone in between (not to mention our democratic discourse as a whole), so I didn't want to risk potentially alienating a conservative audience by revealing my political ideology too soon. Even in doing so, I'm wondering how many people might put down the book here and now just because I come from the opposite side of the political aisle. Almost certainly, I'm also currently drawing the ire of other conservatives for my assumption that they would stop reading information just because it challenged their viewpoints. Whoever you are, I'd like to challenge you to keep reading while keeping my own political biases in mind.

Another possible solution to reducing media bias seeks to not eliminate it entirely, but to put different biases in contrast with each other. This usually takes the format of particular TV shows, radio programs, or podcasts employing two or more hosts from opposite sides of the political aisle. Shows like CNN's Crossfire, Fox's Hannity and Colmes, and others have sought to bridge the political divide while simultaneously presenting both sides of an issue. These types of shows can be successful, as long as they pick two similarly competent hosts. If the two hosts aren't similar enough in their skill sets, the effect can be something of a political straw man attack, where one host is able to paint the other, less competent host as being representative of their broader political ideology. Unfortunately, this is often exactly the point of some of these shows. These shows also require some form of mutual respect between the hosts, and the ability to actually discuss important topics without getting lost in the weeds.

As many of these news shows are essentially debates in nature, it's often difficult to directly present news without getting lost in the argument. Shows like this can very much benefit from being incredibly well-structured, with times for presenting news and separate times for debating the merits of each side of the news. Otherwise, hosts can have difficulty actually presenting news, and might get drawn into the weeds of each others' arguments. More concerning, this type of show only seems to attract a certain type of audience, one who is willing to entertain both sides to begin with, or one who is already relatively aware of their own biases and doesn't want to get sucked into a news vacuum where they only consume media that validates their already confirmed belief systems. If a solution like this hopes to succeed, it will likely need to be a more broadly used strategy across mainstream media networks, rather than just a briefly streamed segment.

Unfortunately, it's rather difficult for the vast majority of the larger cable news networks to incentivize this less partisan environment. Outside of the National Public Radio, which as a publicly funded station is subject to much stricter scrutiny from the American people, news networks are, in theory, able to have a fair amount of freedom when deciding how exactly they want to report the news. The "in theory" carries a lot of weight there. Sure, the repeal of the Fairness Doctrine gives networks agency, but these networks are subjected to outside pressures as well. Let's look at the origins of Fox News and CNN as examples.

Before Fox and CNN arrived on the scene, cable news largely consisted of ABC, CBS, and NBC, each broadcasting for about 30 minutes each night. These three-lettered giants dominated the cable news media for decades, particularly during the era of the Fairness Doctrine. They trended towards the political center, reflecting the less partisan environment of this particular time period. In 1980, a newcomer arrived, changing the news landscape permanently. CNN began as an outsider, even being nicknamed the "Chicken Noodle Network" due to its infancy when compared to the already present giants of media.[89] However, it offered something that other networks could not: constancy. While other networks provided brief, 30 minute segments of news coverage, CNN simply didn't stop. They maintained 24-hour news coverage, instantly responding to news stories as they occurred. The "size" of the news didn't matter, if it showed the slightest bit of relevancy, it could be reported on. Also, it was one of the first news networks to attempt to cover global news, a feat now made possible by the 24-hour news cycle. While CNN's consistency was a major strength in its infancy, it's also important to note that this also established the precedent of constantly following the news that leads to so much news fatigue today. It's likely that somebody would have begun universal coverage eventually, but CNN certainly started the trend that continues to this day. This innovation served the network well, as it became famous for its coverage of international news and elections, becoming a trusted name in war correspondence as well as politics.[90] CNN's dominance in this realm continued, largely without competition, until 1996.

1996 was a huge year for cable news media, sending shockwaves into the industry that still reverberate today. Perhaps a good place to start is the Telecommunications Act of 1996. Among other things, the Telecommunications Act deregulated cable TV services and reduced regulations on media mergers. Time Warner media took advantage of this almost immediately, acquiring CNN. Also carefully watching these developments were media executives Tom Rogers and Rupert Murdoch. Sensing an opening, Tom Rogers founded MSNBC as a younger, more progressive alternative to CNN, with financial backing from Microsoft and General Electric.[91] Also sensing a similar, conservative-shaped opening, Rupert Murdoch swooped in and attempted to purchase CNN. After failing to do so, he created Fox News a few months later as a conservative alternative to MSNBC.[92] In the span of a couple of months, cable news media had expanded from a united front of three, relatively centrist broadcasting organizations to six incredibly variable organizations, at least two of which were created with the explicit intent of counteracting each other. With this history in mind, it's relatively easy to see why major news media is not only as partisan as it is, but also why there's such an incentive to maintain this partisanship over time. In the United States, cable news media appears to have settled into three distinct lanes. According to most media bias charts, media like Fox News fit into the Right lane, MSNBC and CNN fit into the Left and Left Center lane, respectively, and NPR, ABC, CBS, and others fit into the Middle lane.[93] When we look at media in these distinct lanes, we see that the most popular three are consistently Fox, MSNBC, and CNN, with the others falling significantly behind.[94] Even without accounting for political preferences, it's clear that our current media system incentivizes the growing partisanship of these three networks which, due to these incentives, have become the most popularly watched (with Fox dominating conservative-leaning viewership, and MSNBC and CNN splitting liberal-leaning viewership). As long as Fox and MSNBC/CNN are able to dominate the partisan wings, they'll continue to benefit from increased viewership as long as citizens gravitate towards these wings.

Ideally, there are two ways that individuals can significantly reduce this incentive structure of partisanship in the media. The first is controlled mostly by viewers themselves. If the vast majority of TV viewers decide to receive their political news from the less biased sources in the center, partisan media will lose the incentives offered to them from a more biased audience, and they will be forced to move more centrally in order to adapt. An additional benefit to this method is a citizenry who is more educated on both sides of an issue, which will not only decrease partisan hatred, but it should also lead to a more educated general public that can argue about issues without being on an entirely different page from their counterparts. The second way to reduce the incentive structure of partisanship involves a bit more involvement from the media companies themselves. If the amount of media companies were to, say, drastically increase, then the balance of partisan vs centrist news organizations could be regained. If there's an equal number of powerful partisan and centrist news organizations, the benefits of being the "only" major partisan news organizations begin to dissipate. While this can happen organically, it's incredibly unlikely that any new cable news network will be able to displace MSNBC, Fox News, or CNN due to their massive financial and viewership advantages. While I'd certainly prefer more options, it's historically difficult to break up monopolies without government intervention. Still, there are other ways for viewers and news consumers themselves to have some sense of agency in the process. What if instead of attracting viewers to new cable news channels, viewers could be attracted to different mediums of news reporting altogether?

According to recent polling from Pew Research, a whopping 86% of Americans receive news from digital devices, while now only 68% get their news from TV.[95] The media landscape is changing, and newer forms of news proliferation could be pulling the rug out from under the feet of cable media. These forms are already part of most of our daily lives, and can be easily integrated into our daily news diets. They're pretty popular among the young and old alike, however, different forms of it are preferred by different age groups. I'm talking, of course, about social media—the next frontier of news.

Of course, social media in and of itself is something of a field full of landmines. Or, more accurately, a bunch of landmines disguising themselves as a field. Attempting to disseminate journalism on these platforms is no different. Not only have numerous studies shown social media to be a rather inhospitable place for young minds, increasing rates of depression and low self-esteem,[96] but also it can be an inhospitable place for factual information. Studies have shown that roughly 40% of individuals have either knowingly or unknowingly spread "fake news" on social media.[97] Adding to this problem is the notion of exactly how fast false information spreads on social media, especially in comparison to real information. Fake news stories are retweeted 70% more often than real news stories, and fake news reaches large numbers of people (often set at 1,500 in most studies) about six times faster than true news stories do.[98]

It's clear that news on social media has an incredibly long way to go if it hopes to be as viable as more established news networks. Herein lies the major paradox that we face when we look at social media as a legitimate news platform: even though social media can negatively impact the dissemination of news, it has a layout that, if used correctly, could actually prove to be less biased and more accurate than larger partisan media outlets. The phrase "if used correctly" plays a major role in the previous sentence. While social media in its current form is a bastion of fake news, the way it's set up is incredibly conducive to becoming a much more democratic disseminator of news, in strict opposition to the mainstream sources that rely mostly on a profit incentive in order to keep their audiences. What makes Instagram, Facebook, TikTok, podcasts, and other forms of social media so different is that they're largely run by the creators themselves, with only a bit of oversight from the platform's moderators (albeit to a varying degree depending on which platform). This is, of course, both a pro and a con for social media. Social media is set up rather similarly to a free market, in opposition to cable news which is controlled by a handful of monopolies. Theoretically, the better content one produces, the more engagement one will receive compared to competitors, and the more successful they will become. However, this can only just add to the problem. In order to increase viewership, some internet news sources resort to the shock jock, doom and gloom, "we're all going to die" kind of media coverage that pulls in viewers, but doesn't actually make news any more factual or informative. Unfortunately, the large cable news channels have also proven themselves to be relatively adept at adapting to social media, reducing interviews and speeches to bite-sized pieces to be enjoyed by viewers in another format. Even though these news organizations have a rather large advantage in terms of cash flow and name recognition, it's important to recognize that they haven't completely shut out the competition. Independent news sources are able to still thrive on social media, at least more so than on our television screens.

If social media does indeed more resemble a free market of information, it's important to recognize that certain regulations should be in place so that it doesn't go the way of cable news, dominated by a handful of players who are able to rather easily block newcomers out. However, figuring out exactly how to do so wades into an incredibly complex discussion pool regarding freedom of speech on the internet, and particularly the role that social media companies play in it. First, I think that it's important to recognize that first amendment protections regarding freedom of speech do not actually extend to regulation by social media platforms. The first amendment refers to Congress making "no law respecting an establishment of religion, or prohibiting the free exercise thereof; or abridging the freedom of speech, or of the press."[99] Notice that the first amendment only applies to Congress itself, and private organizations certainly are able to abridge freedom of speech or the press if they so choose. Now, of course, the question changes a little bit. If something is legal, does that make it right? In many instances, the answer is not necessarily. There are instances where one's freedom of speech can be abridged by the government if it could cause mortal danger to others, such as screaming "fire" in a movie theater when there is none. Applying these rules to social media is an incredibly nuanced concept, one that we can hopefully find some agreement on. In order to figure out how to adequately and morally do so, I think it's best to have some universal goals in mind that most people can agree on before we decide exactly what to do to make news on social media as accurate as possible. Here's my best stab at what these goals or ideals could be:

1. Everyone benefits from having news sources that are as accurate and unbiased as they can possibly be.
2. We should do everything we can to ensure that all media sources in all forms are publishing accurate information, with the proper context and without omitting useful information that could change the outcome of the story.
3. Any changes we make and any regulation we provide should only exist for the purposes of achieving #1 and #2, and should never be used for the purposes of

amplifying or reducing the voices and views of any individual or group, unless that voice or viewpoint causes or calls for direct harm to another group.

4. Any regulation will be imperfect, and so individuals share some form of personal responsibility in ensuring that the news they consume is indeed accurate, saving the strongest suspicion for the news stories that most confirm their already held points of view.

Let's start with the first rule, as I'm pretty sure it's the most widely accepted. Strictly speaking, a society benefits from when all of its citizens are on the same page, even if they're not necessarily reading the exact same words. Some of the worst forms of partisanship occur when each group is being fed entirely different, contradictory information. While there are cases in which contradictory information can be true, this most commonly occurs when each side is only receiving part of the story. Ensuring that everyone is at least hearing the same story allows us to have differing opinions on the same set of facts, which is much healthier for democracy than disagreeing on the facts in the first place. This leads us to our second point.

The second rule is important in establishing the same set of facts for all involved. Very often, the main reason why people can have such differing opinions are because they're both being presented with entirely opposite, but simultaneously true, sets of facts. While it seems impossible for contradictory sets of facts to be true, it actually happens a lot more often than we might believe. Let's bring it back to our childhoods and say, for example, that children Hayden and Skyler are playing on the playground at recess. They're away from their friends, and Hayden steals a ball from Skyler. In return, Skyler yells at Hayden and pushes them into the mulch. When the two of them talk to their friends, Hayden tells of how Skyler pushed them into the mulch, and Skyler tells of how Hayden stole the ball from them. The pair's friends square up for a fight, only knowing half of the story. While this is a rather juvenile example, it happens all of the time in political dialogue, especially during more violent, chaotic events. People often choose the side that best fits in with their political ideology, and are often even only fed the facts that do just that. It's a recipe for instant partisanship and hatred of the other side, because how on earth could one believe the other side is in the right when the facts so clearly indicate that my side has the moral high ground? Often, both sides are basing their opinions on completely different facts. Consequently, it's incredibly important that media sources are able to tell the whole, entire story, and not just focus on the parts that build up their own side.

Third, it's incredibly important that any regulations on the above aren't used for their own political interests. Here's where things get just a little bit dicey. The current regulations issued by social media sites are implemented by the sites themselves, as they should be. The tools in their toolbox include removing posts, slapping "warning" stickers on others, and temporarily or permanently banning certain accounts. As it probably should be, the bans and removals that occur are pretty explicitly laid out by the social media's rules, which indicate there will be consequences for violence, abuse, terrorism, sexual exploitation, self-harm, sensitive media, and illegal goods or services.[100] Additionally, platforms have pages where they specify what types of misinformation they remove, as well as what exactly they do about it.[101,102] To their credit, Meta and Twitter both explain that they often label posts as being misleading that have been confirmed by a panel of experts as being so, and also often provide the proper context to give the reader the full story of what happened. Unfortunately, to their detriment, misinformation still spreads incredibly rapidly on social media, and these social media sites can often have a heavier hand in banning accounts than they recognize in their rules. Rather than banning posts entirely, it appears as if these sites would benefit from simply seeking to provide the proper context, allowing certain posts to remain as long as they're telling one side of the story, while also telling the other side of the story. You wouldn't be wrong if you thought that this looks relatively similar to the aforementioned

Fairness Doctrine. Returning to a form of this doctrine on social media might indeed prove useful for maintaining factual accuracy, so long as it didn't simultaneously lead to an increase in bans for anything outside of the already established policy. However, there are some cases in which zero tolerance policies should be employed: those who call for and cause direct harm to others, such as accounts aiding and abetting human trafficking, abuse, the selling of illicit drugs, terrorism, hate crimes, and the like.

Finally, it's still important to recognize that absolutely no form of legislation will be absolutely perfect, and any regulation of social media sites, coming from within or without the site, will be no exception. Misinformation will always slip through the cracks, and it will still spread incredibly quickly, often much faster than true information itself. If we want to actually curb the spread of misinformation, then we as a society need to collectively improve at identifying it. Luckily, there are several ways to do so. One of the first and most popular ways is by increasing media literacy. Media literacy is, strictly speaking, formal education in how media works, the incentive structures it faces, and how to differentiate true facts from false information. Hopefully this chapter has been a relatively good start on increasing your own media literacy, but there are far better, more structured ways of doing so as well. Another popular way of doing so is through the implementation of media literacy classes in schools. As of the time of this book, 14 states have passed laws elevating student education in media literacy, which is especially important considering that this skill is one that can be learned from a young age.[103] While media literacy classes are gaining traction in classrooms, there are also online resources that I would highly recommend accessing at the Newseum website,[104] as well as a shorter lesson designed for kids by PBS.[105] I'll summarize some of the tips they share, as well as some of my own, in my first, and likely only, iteration of:

Matthew's Media Literacy Medley

1. **Always check for sources**

No matter what, the absolute most important thing to check is whether news media cites their sources for every single claim. This goes for books (including this one), newspapers, social media sites, anything. If there are no sources, there should be no claim. If the sources are biased, take claims with a grain of salt. Reuters, the Associated Press, and NPR tend to be rated among the least biased, but even these are far from perfect.

2. **Look for keywords**

Very rarely does something "always" or "never" happen. If claims like these are made, the author needs to be absolutely certain that it is indeed always or never the case, with no exceptions. Similarly, if an author uses loaded or emotional words, they're more likely to be trying to make you feel a particular reaction, rather than actually demonstrating a valid point. While this isn't necessarily a bad thing for more artistic pieces, or for events that are indeed emotionally laden, it's not necessarily appropriate for most editorial level news. Additionally, if the writing elicits an emotional reaction, you're less likely to be able to evaluate it logically.

3. **Be a conscious consumer of information**

This is sometimes a particularly difficult one. There's so much going on at every moment of our lives that we often skim through news stories, perhaps only looking at the headlines before moving on. Unfortunately, headlines can often be the least true part of the news story, as they're designed to grab your attention and direct your clicks to the story itself. If you choose to read something, try to take the time to slow down and consider it fully. Does it make sense with what you know? Does anything stand out as sounding fake or incorrect? Do other media sources corroborate all parts of the story?

4. **Know yourself, especially your own biases**

This is often another difficult task. Even if we know ourselves very well, it's difficult to recognize when we bring our own biases to a news story. We're incredibly likely to pay attention to things that we already agree with, but recognizing what you're already likely to believe can make it that much easier to keep yourself in check.

5. **Read and watch what you disagree with as often as what you agree with**

Yes, I know, it's not always fun to read something that you completely disagree with. In fact, it's never an easy task. However, reading and watching things you disagree with regularly will allow you to look at things from a slightly different perspective, and more importantly, challenge the biases that you hold. After all, you really want your views to be as strong as possible. Regularly engaging with content you disagree with can help you to understand which of your views you can easily defend and stand by, and which ones might require a little bit more nuance. Challenge yourself, and see what happens. Another way of doing this is by having conversations with people you know you'll disagree with. Having respectful conversations with people you disagree with helps you understand your more and less defensible viewpoints, and it allows you to experience disagreement with a real person, rather than an easily vilified private account online.

While these tips and tricks can help you manage many different situations, social media has already begun to evolve in a way that might mitigate some of these newfound skills. In particular, the algorithmic equations popularized by TikTok and Youtube and adopted by Instagram and Facebook Reels, which recommends future content to users based on their previous engagement with content, is somewhat problematic for avoiding biases in one's scrolling habits. Unfortunately, when people "like," or simply spend more time watching videos from a particular political group, they will be recommended similar videos from similar political groups in the future. While this is convenient from a viewing perspective, it's an incredibly easy way for individuals to fall into their own tailor-made echo chambers where they only really view content that validates their already held viewpoints. One possible solution would be for companies to alter their algorithms so that instead of receiving similar videos from a particular political ideology, individuals simply receive political content in general. Hopefully, this would reduce the echo in individuals' echo chambers by exposing them to a variety of political content, however this would require social media companies to alter their algorithms, which might not be conducive to their business model which profits on people staying in their own political echo chambers.

Investigating the causes and solutions of media bias is an ongoing process, and one with no easy answer. Disagreement is an important part of democracy, but disagreement can only be helpful if everyone is basing their viewpoints on the same set of shared facts. Otherwise, partisan polarization is pretty inevitable, as is increasing distrust and hatred between each party. Regrettably, many of our news organizations have found our disagreements to be financially profitable, and indeed rely on furthering these divisions in order to keep ratings high. Regardless of what you think of candidates like Donald Trump, it's hard to deny that his brashness and polarizing speeches were fantastic for cable news ratings. A financial incentive permeates our political system, from our politicians to our news organizations. In order to truly create some form of democracy, terminating these financial incentives would be a great place to start.

Chapter 9: Financial Incentives

In theory, a democracy is meant to be controlled by the will of the people, and the will of the people alone. Although the form of democracy has changed radically over time, you'll find that the vast majority of systems based in democracy still strive to follow this basic rule, as well as the rule that each person gets one vote. This is the basis of democracy, and is one of the reasons why this form of government has been able to survive for so long, even if certain methods of its representation have been changed. It is this "one person, one vote" concept that makes democracies so enduring, as they always strive to represent the will of the individuals they govern.

A major benefit of democracy is that it is incredibly responsive to this will. If a law is passed or a representative is elected that goes against the will of the people at large, theoretically, the democracy will be able to overturn that law or remove that public official. Its responsiveness and reactivity allows it to grow and change over time along with the growth and change that its population experiences over time. As citizens go through war, peace, economic boom and bust, periods of plenty and periods of little, so does the democracy flex and bend to meet citizens' ever changing needs. The concept of democracy has been a dominant governmental force for thousands of years now, and without this responsiveness to the people, without its ability to change over time, it likely would not survive. There's a reason why dictatorships today are so few and far between, and why they require immense amounts of propaganda and seclusion from the outside world in order to avoid revolutions and repercussions.

The government of America in the early 1800s resembles its government today, but the bills and laws that the same government produces, as well as the people who participate in it, are now incredibly different. Additionally, even though America has maintained something of a one-person one-vote system (even after it has been diluted by the Senate and the Electoral College), there have been other, extra-governmental factors at play that shape the results of its elections. The concept of one-person one-vote works fantastically in theory, but votes alone are but one factor that influences the outcome of elections. One of the other major factors, of course, is money.

While it has arguably taken center stage rather recently, the concept of financial incentives pervading politics is one that's been present for a while in American democracy, but one that might seem completely alien to the Founding Fathers. You see, even the concept of using outside groups to fund campaigns didn't exist until Andrew Jackson in 1829, as candidates often funded their own campaigns—a much easier feat than it would be nowadays due to a lack of advertisements. In what would likely be the earliest display of campaigning, George Washington (and others) would offer free whiskey in exchange for votes, a process that would be more than a little bit illegal today. Going back to Jackson, it appears that his campaign represented one of the first larger scale "campaigns" in American history. A man with little prestige or personal wealth upon his birth, Jackson rose through the ranks and eventually became a congressman, senator, and general prior to his election as president. Creating the first grassroots campaign, he traveled the country and used the primitive media in order to advertise his candidacy, although he also didn't collect campaign funds from potential voters. Jackson's candidacy and presidency may have established the precedent of campaigning for public office, but the campaigning process still had a long ways to go after his first campaign succeeded.[106] Likely the most influential (and most detrimental) addition to our political system so far came almost 60 years after Jackson's first campaign: the political machine.

It's not too terribly often that a term means exactly what you would think it means, but a political machine comes pretty darn close. Strictly speaking, political machines were begun so that one could put voters in one end and extract votes from them (cast, of course, for the machine's intended candidate) by the time they came out the other side. At first glance, these machines didn't seem to be too terribly insidious. Many of them functioned by working with voters to solve problems at the local level, providing housing, jobs, sanitation, childcare, food, and other needs. However, all of this help came at a cost: the individuals helped would pledge to vote for the machine's candidate of choice in the next election. These machines worked hand in hand with some of the most corrupt politicians who sought to stay in power no matter what, regardless of whether or not they were actually working to better the lives of their constituents. More often than not, they weren't, but they successfully used the machine to gain re-election. Usually the system looked something like this:

> **Step 1-** Corrupt politicians pass laws that enrich themselves while making the lives of their voters worse.
> **Step 2-** Voters either get angry at the corrupt politicians, or aren't even made aware of any events happening due to said corruption.
> **Step 3-** The corrupt politicians' machine steps in, helping to fix the problem that the politician created in the first place. . . all for the simple price of pledged loyalty at the polls.
> **Step 4-** Afraid of the repercussions, citizens vote for the candidate that the machine indicates, and the corrupt politicians become re-elected once again.

As you can see, the plan was simple, yet genius, in its insidiousness. Allowing the machine itself to solve the problems that its corruption had created kept voters constantly indebted to the machine. Also, a lack of transparency between government officials might even keep the politicians' misdeeds secret from their constituents, reducing any indication that they're trapped in a constant cycle of dependency.[107] This doesn't even begin to recognize the fact that many individuals in this cycle were only nominated to political office in the first place because of their loyalty to the political machine. Oh, and of course we can't forget that some machines would hire people to vote several different times, paying off sheriffs to look the other way. One of the more prominent and egregious machines was the William "Boss" Tweed Ring in New York City, also known as Tammany Hall. Their résumé of electoral and legal missteps is so large and long that it honestly might just be best to list them all together at the same time:

-Allowed the wealthy and the middle class to escape the draft by paying 300 dollars
-Paid off judges for favorable rulings
-Had construction officials overcharge for hospitals, courthouses, museums, roads, and bridges, with the extra funding going back to Tweed directly
-Bought up the printing company that produced ballots to make them more favorable to party members
-Bought a huge amount of real estate to rent out to citizens
-Gave away most public official jobs due to patronage, rather than merit
-Bribed or arrested election officials who questioned people voting more than once
-Stuffed ballot boxes with fake votes
-Falsified election results entirely
-Used thugs or crooked cops to sway the minds of voters and intimidate them

-Bribed news reporters to not print stories of his corruption
And so much more![108]

Surprisingly enough, "Boss" Tweed was actually arrested in 1871 and sentenced to 12 years in prison, but not before his machine brought in nearly 200 million dollars (or almost five billion dollars today) in corrupt money. While his machine finally broke down, as did the last of the political machines by the early 1940s,[109] the role of money in politics was just taking form, albeit in a slightly more insidious way.

Almost at the exact moment that the last political machine broke down, its successor entered the political stage for the first time ever: the Political Action Committee, or PAC. Up until that point, the party itself was the primary megaphone for candidates and party officials. However, as the failures of the party machine began to expose holes in the strength of the party system itself, and as parties began to lose their stranglehold on the American electorate, some decided that political messaging might be best invested in a mechanism outside of the parties themselves. From the beginning, PACs were sleek, new ways to make changes in politics. They raised money by collecting donations from the electorate, then they would turn around and spend that money on advertisements for a particular candidate, party, or issue. They often had media experts at their disposal, individuals whose jobs were to make sure that political messaging was as concise and as powerful as it possibly could be. Additionally, PACs became necessary as an outlet for funding after a 1907 prohibition stopped labor organizers, trades, and special interests from donating directly to parties. Instead, they could now donate to Political Action Committees, which could in turn run advertisements for candidates. These rules stayed more or less in place until the 1970s, when a flurry of changes established the 1971 Federal Election Campaign Act (FECA), which provided limits on candidate spending on broadcasting as well as increased transparency in reporting what campaigns were actually spending their money on. In the wake of Watergate, the Federal Election Commission, or FEC, was established in order to enforce the Federal Election Campaign Act. These legal and procedural changes set the scene for today's battleground for campaign finance, which arguably begins with the 1976 Supreme Court case of Buckley v. Valeo.[106]

Here's where things start to get interesting, and our current political landscape begins to be shaped. Let's start with Buckley v. Valeo. In this Supreme Court case, Senator Buckley from New York attempted to make the case that the Federal Election Campaign Act was unconstitutional because money is an expression of free speech. Following this logic, curtailing the amount that an individual could spend on a candidate, as well as the amount that a candidate could spend on their own campaign was a violation of the free speech protected by the first amendment. After deliberation, the court found that limitations on contributions to candidates for public office were indeed legal, as these limits helped to serve the greater purpose of maintaining the fairness of elections, and ensuring that any one individual wasn't able to have an oversized impact on their outcomes. However, this court also struck down the limits that individuals could donate to their *own* campaign, because contributing to one's own campaign didn't enhance the potential for corruption, as these contributions were money that one was essentially burning for their own political interests.[110]

So, for those of you keeping score at home, campaign finance in the late 1970s looks something like this:

> Can individuals donate anything they want to any campaign? **NO**
> Can individuals donate anything they want to their own campaign? **YES**
> Can individuals, businesses, parties, and other organizations donate anything they want to PACs: **No, only under 5,000 dollars at this point**

After Buckley v. Valeo, the next major campaign finance decision came through the Legislative branch. In 2002, Russ Feingold and John McCain worked together to create the Bipartisan Campaign Reform Act. This act in particular focused largely on soft money, or money donated to PACs and other political organizations (as opposed to hard money, which is directly donated to candidates). This act prohibited party soft money donations to candidates, and also tied contribution limits to inflation, largely reiterating the legal solutions arrived at by the Buckley v. Valeo decision. It also added the "Stand by your ad" provision, which is largely why you hear so many political advertisements today which claim "I'm [insert candidate here], and I approve this message," as long as the advertisement came directly from the campaign.[111] The McCain-Feingold Act experienced some troubles after it was passed, and in 2007, it was ruled that groups could indeed use corporate or union contributions to run political advertisements, so long as they didn't explicitly endorse the candidate. Of course, this led to negative advertisements against the ideology of other candidates, as well as ads promoting particular issues, so long as they didn't promote the candidate or party itself. To slightly update the score sheet, it looks something like this:

> Can individuals donate anything they want to any campaign? **NO**
> Can individuals donate anything they want to their own campaign? **YES**
> Can individuals, businesses, parties, and other organizations donate anything they want to PACs: **No, only under 5,000 dollars directly to PACs (adjusted for inflation). However, these PACs can spend whatever they want on running ads that aren't directly connected to a candidate or party.**

Now, this all seems to be making reasonable sense so far. As time has progressed, campaign finance laws have similarly progressed, reducing the financial influences of groups as compared to the individual. This was the golden era for campaign finance laws if you will, where they had the most influence on election integrity, and had found the largest amount of bipartisan success so far. Of course, this was all about to change.

In 2010, the Supreme Court heard Citizens United v. the Federal Elections Commission. After their advertisement against Hillary Clinton's primary campaign was blocked by the FEC, conservative nonprofit Citizens United took their case to the Supreme Court, making the argument that blocking such an advertisement violated their first amendment rights. In contrast to the previous ruling in Buckley v. Valeo, the Supreme Court ruled that in this case, the previously established anti-corruption measures validating the cap on spending didn't apply, and that any worries about corruption would subsequently be questioned by a company's shareholders and reversed through something they called "corporate democracy." Inherently, Citizens United ruled that since companies were made up of people (their shareholders), their political donations should be treated as such, and that corporate expenditures could not be limited.[112] This essentially reclassified corporations as having the same protections as human beings, at least under campaign finance law. The decision was 5-4. Additionally, the 2014 Supreme Court Case McCutcheon v. FEC used the previous precedent set by Citizens United v. FEC to further erode campaign finance laws. After McCutcheon wished to contribute more than the biennial limit permitted, the Supreme Court held that a biennial limit was unconstitutional, and removed the overall cap on individual contributions entirely, except for those directly to a candidate. So, finally, at this point in time, our scorecard looks something like this[113]:

> Can individuals donate anything they want to any campaign? **Kind of, there's an individual limit for *each* candidate, but no limit for the number of candidates.**

Can individuals donate anything they want to their own campaign? **YES**
Can individuals, businesses, parties, and other organizations donate anything they want to PACs: **YES**

As you can see, this is starting to become slightly more grim. Don't worry, it gets worse. After the decisions of Citizens United and McCutcheon v. FEC came some of the most troubling inventions in the modern era of campaign finance: dark money and the Super PAC. As these decisions stripped the FEC of much of their enforcement powers, their ability to stop unknown campaign contributions dissolved to virtually nothing. After Citizens United in particular, dark money began to play a role in American elections. Strictly speaking, dark money is election spending with no clear source. Dark money can't be traced, and because of this, it can be spent almost endlessly, as the FEC has no power to track and stop it. After Citizens United, the amount of dark money spent on elections ballooned in size, and now represents the largest contributions to elections in the United States. Additionally, the results of these Supreme Court cases allowed for the creation of a newer, more insidious form of Political Action Committee: the Super PAC.

The name Super PAC seems born from a Marvel comic book, but it's no joke. This upgraded, supercharged version of the Political Action Committee has played an ever-increasing role in federal, state, and even local elections since their inception. Largely, they came into being after yet another court ruling immediately following Citizens United: SpeechNOW.org v. FEC. The website SpeechNOW.org was and is a company that pools together funding from individuals to spend on elections, attempting to streamline the collective action problem faced by people who wish to affect an election or issue, but can't make change happen by themselves. In particular, they took issue with the previous precedent established by the FECA regarding independent expenditures. Independent expenditures are those types of political ads that express support or disdain for a candidate, but don't work directly with the candidate or his/her party. Previous FECA precedents had set a cap of donations from any one individual to organizations such as these, and SpeechNOW made the similar argument that such caps violated their first amendment rights. I believe you can see the trend here, but the D.C. Court of Appeals, leaning on the Supreme Court's precedent set in McCutcheon v. FEC and Citizens United v. FEC, issued a similar ruling. The D.C. Court of Appeals ruled that in addition to limits on spending, limits on contributions to private organizations such as SpeechNOW were indeed unconstitutional, and in violation of the first amendment.[114] Now, for the first time, individuals can donate unlimited funding to these types of organizations, now branded as Super Political Action Committees (or sometimes known as independent expenditure-only committees, or Super PACs) due to their size and scope. Now, as long as the Super PAC itself doesn't donate money directly to the candidate or their party, they can take in unlimited amounts of money from as many or as few donors as it wants, and spend it on the candidate or policy initiative of their choice.[115]

It's fair to say that this decision sent shockwaves through the political sphere. Not only does it open up the possibility for the ultra wealthy to play an increasingly large role in the political system, it also spits in the face of the McCain-Feingold Act that required candidates to stand by their own personal advertisements. While these personally-curated advertisements still exist, there's room for outside forces to craft their own political advertisements for or against candidates at will. This spells trouble for democracy in more ways than one. The first ill effect is the rather obvious one. If Super PACs have theoretically unlimited funding (as long as they're able to secure donors), political races begin to turn into financial horse races, with the biggest spender often becoming the biggest winner. In 2020, the House candidate with more funding won 87% of the time, while better funded Senate candidates won 71% of the time.[116] Regardless of candidate quality, spending and fundraising has become a much larger part of running a campaign. From 2000 to 2020, spending on presidential elections almost tripled, rising from

4.1 billion dollars to 10.9 billion dollars.[117] Additionally, as spending increases and candidates benefit more from billionaire donors, candidates spend more time courting high-dollar donors at more expensive fundraisers, simply because of the financial incentives established by these rulings. This means that businesses have even more incentive to hire lobbyists, or individuals whose sole purpose is to schmooze politicians, often offering hefty donations in exchange for the politician's support of a desired policy. Now a world where campaign funding is unlimited leads to candidates who are more receptive to the wants and needs of their donors, who are unfortunately becoming wealthier and wealthier.

The other major ill effect of this ruling is just as insidious, but slightly less obvious. If candidates aren't required to stand behind advertisements created by Super PACs, it makes it that much harder to run fair, honorable elections. Prior to the 2010 ruling, if a candidate wanted to run a negative advertisement against their opponent, they then had to stand next to the advertisement on live TV and say that they approved this message. Inherently, in addition to taking a pot shot at their opponent, this also showed voters that this candidate very much approved of said pot shot, which could cost them points among voters who want politics to be slightly less vicious and gruesome. But by incentivizing Super PACs to create advertisements of their own with much more funding, a candidate can leave the negative advertising to the Super PACs, while focusing on deflecting blows from their opponent or highlighting their record in their own campaign messaging. In this case, rather than standing by their aggression, a candidate is able to simply reply, "What ad? Oh, that must have just been a Super PAC, I had no hand in that" whenever they're questioned about a particularly egregious advertisement. Unfortunately, this scheme leads to more negative and polarizing elections overall, as candidates are able to stay high and dry as their Super PACs duke it out in the trenches. Because of this, there's an incentive for people to join politics who are able to mentally withstand a malicious smear campaign. A key effect of this is drastically reducing the number of people who want to get involved in politics. I mean, if you're reading this book, it's likely that you've at least entertained the notion of jumping into politics at some point in your life. You have good ideas, you have some solutions to problems, and I mean hey, you could definitely do better than a lot of the idiots in there, right? You're probably absolutely correct, to be honest.

The way that the system is set up currently benefits those who can take that moral or personal hit, and there are certainly a lot of people who have avoided running for public office because of those same problems. Unfortunately, that's not quite where the problems end for our electoral system. Even though Citizens United and SpeechNOW kept the provision in place that required PACs and Super PACs to report their donors, this isn't always the case. Some organizations are actually able to get around this requirement, and don't have to disclose where their money comes from.

I'll try not to get too into the weeds, as much of this stuff is incredibly technical to the point of incomprehension, but many of these problems stem from a certain type of nonprofit called a 501(c)(4), which is an untaxed nonprofit that can donate to Super PACs and can offer endorsements of political candidates. There's one catch, however. The express purpose of the 501(c)(4) needs to be advocating for some kind of *social* change, not *political* change. These rules are abused just about as often as you would think they would be. As supposedly (but often not in reality) apolitical nonprofit organizations, these organizations are allowed to remain anonymous in their donations, and *don't need to report their donations* to Super PACs.[118] This exchange is known as dark money, or money that doesn't have a known donor or receiver. Not only do 501(c)(4)s not need to report their donations, Super PACs don't (or sometimes can't) report which 501(c)(4) donated to them. Some examples of the most powerful 501(c)(4)s are the National Rifle Association (NRA), VoteVets.org, Americans for Constitutional Liberty, Third Way, and Turning Point Action. Many of these organizations are rather large spenders, and often have very political missions. Their dark money can heavily influence the winners of elections, while voters might not even know where the money is coming from or how it's being spent. Dark money makes up about 100-200 million dollars in campaign funding each cycle, but there's a silver lining hidden in this dark cloud.

Dark money hit its peak in the 2012 election, with 300 million dollars in undisclosed donations spent, but that number has been slowly shrinking since then. The 2020 election only saw a bit over 100 million dollars in undisclosed funding, a significant decrease.[119] While I can only speculate as to why dark money continues to have a decreasing role in election funding, I can imagine that it's because voters have become smarter and more well informed. If a candidate is known to receive a large proportion of their funding from undisclosed sources, then voters aren't aware of who the candidate is likely to be loyal to upon election. It's possible that this influence of dark money can shrink in the future. If voters are able to become more aware of which candidates are receiving funding from undisclosed sources, they can filter these candidates out of the primary and general election process. This is where voters are able to reclaim some agency that has been previously lost by loosening campaign finance laws. While we're a flawed democracy, voters still do have power. If enough people become aware of the dark money flowing into campaigns, then those candidates can be taken down, and dark money can become a thing of the past—just a blight on a candidate's record rather than a tool to win elections.

So, how do we fix this system? It might be just about time for:

Matthew's Methods to Mash Money in Politics

(This is the last one I promise)

1. **Inform and Educate Voters**

The first solution falls strictly into the hands of the voters. As much as you can, do your research, and look at the organizations that are funding your candidate options. If a candidate receives more funding from undisclosed sources, or more funding from lobbyists hoping to sway their vote in a way that would be helpful for their particular industry, maybe it would be a good idea to be slightly more wary of checking their name at the ballot box. The website OpenSecrets.org has a fair amount of good resources for tracking campaign donations, and might be a good place to start for individuals hoping to learn more about where their candidates' funding comes from. The more you know, the better decisions you'll be able to make. This one's up to you.

2.   **Repeal Citizens United v. FEC, McCutcheon v. FEC, and SpeechNOW.org v. FEC**

This one is unfortunately significantly harder, as it's incredibly difficult to re-litigate a Supreme Court or District Court case. Additionally, the makeup of the court (as of 2023 at least) is unlikely to attempt to relitigate this case. However, if you remember from the chapter regarding the Judicial branch, the Supreme Court has experienced a massive drop in approval in recent years. If the court hopes to gain favor in the national spotlight, it might be time to make another ruling that would increase the effectiveness of voting again and reduce the power of special interests.

3.   **Introduce legislation to perform the above through Congress**

In 2021, House Democrats introduced the For the People Act, a bill that could drastically change campaign finance and rewrite some of the decisions made under the previous Supreme Court cases. If the changes did indeed hold up in court, the For the People Act sought to ban foreign money in elections, reduce the influence of shell companies that allow foreign money into elections, disclose who pays for online political ads, create a federal donation matching system for small dollar donations (that's you), require political organizations to reveal their large donors, and restructure the FEC to have five commissioners (instead of the current six, three Democrats and three Republicans) to avoid gridlock.[120] The bill faces a rather uphill climb, but might just go a long way towards restoring campaign finance laws that have been eroded in the past 20 years or so.

Regardless of what solution you favor, I believe that it's hard to argue that at the very least, increased transparency is absolutely necessary in order to curtail the role of money in our political system. For now, our elections are affected by financial contributions just as much as the votes of citizens. If we truly want America to resemble a democracy, it's up to us to make it so. Politicians have made it clear that they aren't going to do it for us, so it's up to us, the ordinary citizens, to get involved and take back our political power.

Chapter 10: Where do I Fit In?

So, you've made it. You've gotten through a fair amount of history about why the U.S. Government works how it does, as well as quite a bit of commentary about how it could run better. So, where does that leave us? Where do we fit into this story, and what can we do to change the trajectory of the country, to bring the United States ever closer towards that democracy of the people, by the people, and for the people? The answer is one for you yourself to solve as much as it is anyone else's. How has any change in any government ever been made? People, often ordinary citizens clamoring for change and justice, have provided the most rapid, lasting change. The way you work towards the change you want is up to you. Yes, of course that's a cop-out answer. There are so many ways to create change, and each one is specifically tailored to what exactly it is that you want to do. Different people have different talents, which are conducive to fighting for different ideals in different ways. However, as we saw in the chapter on collective action, there are certain ways that individuals can enact the largest amount of change possible. Finding exactly what that is involves finding the intersection between your own particular skills and what you can do with those skills to influence the hearts and minds of those around you. Some people are gifted orators, and are more likely to use their skills of rhetoric to convince people through debate. Others stand out better with the written word, and the precision of prose allows them to problem solve as efficiently as possible. While nobody can choose your path for you, it's sometimes nice to have most of the paths laid out for you so that you know which options you can choose. That's what I hope this book, and specifically this chapter, is able to do for you. Now that we can agree on at least some of the problems, it's time to determine exactly what role we can play in their solution. For our purposes, I'll start with some of the easier steps, which can be started as early as the moment you finish reading. Of course, from there I'll increase the amount of time necessary until we get to those actions that require years of practice and even financial and mental preparation (namely, running for office yourself). So, here we go. Best of luck to you on your journey.

1. **Research.**

Check. Just by reading a book about politics, you're already starting to accomplish one of the best things that you can possibly do. Educating yourself about your country's system of government, as well as its histories, successes, flaws, and goals is by far the best way to introduce yourself into the world of political advocacy. I think it goes without saying that it's difficult to change something you know next to nothing about, and performing research on the topic is one of the best ways of ensuring you know exactly what change you want to make. Unfortunately, politics often isn't quite that easy. There are so many problems, and even more possible solutions, so it's often almost impossible to know where to start looking. In this case, I would recommend starting with one particular issue, your "pet" issue. It can be something that's near and dear to your heart, or a problem you have a particularly unique solution for, or really anything you want. Perhaps start your research with that particular issue. Educate yourself on it as much as possible, until you're reasonably knowledgeable about the issue and how it's seen in the political realm. Have there been attempts to address this issue before? What political snags have the people trying to solve it hit? Looking through the lens of one issue that you understand well helps you to further understand how the political system as a whole affects that one issue. Additionally, you'll likely find out through enough research that that particular issue is tied to other issues as well. These connected issues can be a fantastic place to expand your knowledge, and see where other issues connect to the ones that affect you most. Soon, you'll have a reasonably good knowledge of how the political system works, by looking through the lens of several issues that you know reasonably well. You'll be able to talk about them with others, and have reasonably well-researched opinions on them when they're brought up in conversations. You might even have discovered some solutions as well, which will allow yourself to find candidates and groups who are advocating for similar solutions. This is how a political identity is born, which leads almost immediately into the second possibility:

2. **Have some conversations**

As you undoubtedly know, political conversations can sometimes suck. Like, really suck. Like, Grandpa Antoine disowning Aunt Beth at Thanksgiving because of her ideology suck. Why does political discourse often end this way? While the example is somewhat hyperbolic, I think that political conversations can go this way because we don't have enough practice in disagreeing with people. As seen in the News and the Media chapter, politics is a unique field because people with differing ideologies often believe in different versions of facts. And, because of the way stories are told about events, both sides can come away from the same event with entirely different, but completely true, versions of the event. Even if people are on the same page factually, our politics are so linked to our personalities and self-concept that any disagreement feels more like a personal attack than simply a counterpoint. This, of course, unfortunately doesn't always bode well for political conversation. In order to fix this, it can sometimes be a good idea to look at political conversations as a test of ideas, rather than a personal attack. You have your own thoughts and ideas about a particular policy, as does the other individual, and engaging in respectful political discussion can be incredibly healthy for not only strengthening or modifying one's own ideology, testing out how their ideas fair when matching up against others, but by respectfully listening to another's point of view. It can help two individuals establish a shared set of facts, even if they disagree on how they feel about those facts. In these instances, political discussions should be seen as learning opportunities, where one is able to figure out where the other person comes from, and how their background, upbringing, and likes and dislikes have shaped the person they are today, both politically and in terms of personality.

Now of course, I don't want to skip over the fact that some political "disagreements" are indeed personal attacks disguised as ideology. Some disagreements are much more than just disagreements, particularly when these disagreements relate to one's identity as a human being. Sure, on issues of economic or social policy there can be kind disagreements, but these political disagreements should never extend to who a person is or who they want to be. These conversations verge away from the political and into the personal, and can easily become more of ad hominem arguments, where the person is attacked rather than their particular beliefs. Having these difficult conversations can do a lot to change the hearts and minds of those around you, but if you're beginning to feel personally attacked rather than engaged in a discussion between equals, it's probably a good idea to disengage and try another tactic instead.

3. **Find what you're good at**

One of the many wonders of the human species is that we all have our strengths, and that these strengths are incredibly variable from person to person. Well, the same goes in the political realm. Some of us are better writers, some are better speakers, and some are better at the interpersonal cooperation that goes with organizing. Here is where it's important to figure out whatever it is that you're good at, and stick with it. For myself, that looks like writing. I would consider my writing to be a strength (whether or not it actually is, I suppose is up to you), and so I've found for myself a particular niche in political writing. For me, it started with a fun little site called Quora. For those of you who are unfamiliar, Quora is a question-answer site (not too terribly dissimilar from Yahoo Answers), where individuals are able to ask questions regarding any topic, and crowdsource answers, which are shared, liked, disliked, and commented on in a public forum. Additionally, Quora has what they call "Spaces," or areas devoted to certain topics, followed by individuals interested in said topics. After a bit of time as an answer writer for Quora, I found my niche in a couple of the more political corners. I would write answers on a wide variety of political subjects, pretentiously calling myself an "armchair political scientist." It's always fun to shudder at the mistakes of your former self. While I would at least hope that I have become less pretentious with time, I found a nice little following on Quora, and decided that I really enjoyed writing about the issues that I believed in most, as well as occasionally throwing out decently researched Electoral College predictions for the 2020 election (which didn't end up too badly, if I do say so myself). From there, I decided to combine my time spent on Quora with pursuits in the "real" world, writing Op-Eds and submitting them to various local and national newspapers. While I received somewhere around 30 rejections, I did end up getting an Op-Ed published in the Kansas City Star, which was incredibly gratifying. From there, I just continued to write more and more, and here I am, writing a halfway decent book about something I love talking about that might just help democracy flourish just the slightest bit longer. I hope. What I'm saying here is, if I can do it, anyone can. I'm no political scientist, armchair or otherwise, I'm just someone who believes in improving the laws that we live under, and I use my passion for writing to do just that. It might not be writing, but I have a hunch each and every one of you reading this book are good at something, and that something gives you a political voice. Perhaps you're a fantastic artist who enjoys painting natural scenes to encourage conservation, or you're a spokesperson who could organize the people at your workplace to fight for fairer wages. Everyone has their piece to say and their way to say it, and if you get anything at all from this book, it's that you should take the time to say it. Life's short, and we only have so much time to leave our mark.

4. **Get involved outside of the political system**

No matter how pro-democracy I've been throughout this book, it's worthy of note that, unfortunately, democracies are only as "good" as the politicians that make them up and the citizens who elect them into office. Many rather despicable things have been done under democracies, and these can have horrible impacts on less represented populations who have an undersized impact on the policy that actually gets passed. With this, we need to recognize that democracies, even good ones that give as much power to the people as possible, don't always provide the best solutions. Unfortunately, the majority rule function of democracy can be a double-edged sword. If the majority of a population can be convinced of a policy that would benefit them at the expense of the minority, there's little that can be done to stop them electorally. This concept was very much on the mind of the framers of the United States's constitution, and is a major reason why institutions such as a Senate and filibuster to protect the rights of states are in place. Throughout this book, I've questioned whether these institutions actually protect minorities, or simply hinder necessary progress. Regardless of where you fall, these institutions, particularly the filibuster, have indeed hindered the process of civil rights legislation throughout the course of the history of the United States. Because of this, there is very much extra-governmental work to be done to solve the problems that we face. Democracy and government is just one possible solution, but that doesn't mean that private citizens don't have an immense role to play in their own lives. Non-governmental organizations like nonprofits, community centers, co-ops, churches, and trade unions can be incredibly effective in solving problems, as can more government-focused interventions like protests, walkouts, sit-ins, and civil disobedience to prove the immorality of a particular law. These organizations and actions have a lower buy-in than working for the government directly, and I would say that most people reading this have an easy way to get involved at their workplace, where they regularly shop, or even in their own neighborhood. There are so many ways inside and outside politics to make a positive difference, and hopefully number three can provide you with some place to start.

5. **Run for office yourself**

I said that I was saving the most difficult for last, right? While running for office yourself is by far the hardest action item on this list, it's actually at least a little bit more accessible than you might at first believe, and arguably much more gratifying. It's first important to know that there are so many different levels of elected office, and it's incredibly rare that one's first political job is in Washington, D.C., unless you've become a congressional staffer. However, there are some small, local positions that you could probably run for as early as tomorrow, provided you have the time to fill out some paperwork and talk to some neighbors. Additionally, the rewards are often sweeter at the local level. Not only are these positions much easier to achieve, but also you'll be able to have a rather large and noticeable impact on your community as a whole, all while building your political résumé to potentially run for higher offices.

One such position is called the Precinct Chairperson. These people, elected alongside other local elected officials, act as something of a party representative for each precinct, which can be as small as a few neighborhoods, or even parts of a neighborhood. This person acts as a go-between for those who live in the precinct and the party as a whole, hearing concerns and thoughts of the voters you represent, and attempting to get as many of them to vote for your political party as possible. It's relatively likely that this position is actually empty, or that the current officeholder could be convinced to leave if someone else wanted to pick up the torch badly enough. Either way, this position requires very little campaigning outside of talking to neighbors, and is a relatively easy one for a first time office holder to succeed in.

Above the Precinct Chairperson position are the positions on school boards, city councils, mayoral offices, and other smaller governmental organizations. Depending on the size of your town, this position could either be really easy or really hard to obtain. In incredibly small towns, you could win a mayoral race by just choosing to run for it (or by being a particularly cute dog, which is the case in about nine towns across the U.S.).[121] It costs an estimated 8,000-12,000 dollars in campaign funding to win these races in smaller or medium cities, meaning that fundraising will not necessarily be a walk in the park, but it will be much easier than winning any sort of state-wide race.[122] Additionally, these positions might require a number of signed petitions to get on the ballot, making campaigning more of a time-suck if you need to canvas several neighborhoods yourself in order to just be eligible. Another added benefit of winning local office is the immediate impact you have on the place in which you live. While larger offices can have broader, more impactful effects overall, I can imagine there's no feeling like seeing the town you live in steadily improve, and knowing that you played a small role in helping it along.

At the next level is state senator or representative. Depending on the state you live in, these positions (along with certain mayoral positions) can start to represent full time jobs, and require similar amounts of time from you. After all, you're a legislator now, and will need to travel at least biannually to your state's capital for long periods of time in order to accomplish your legislative duties. This is getting closer to the big time now, and the requirements for winning office reflect that. Sometimes the bill to get on the ballot alone can equal thousands of dollars, and campaigns get significantly more expensive from there, as state senators and state representatives need to cover a lot more ground than local town or city candidates. At this point, it might be worth looking into having a small campaign headquarters and at least a couple permanent staff, which can be a quick drain on resources. However, if you're able to weather the financial storm, securing that sweet, sweet State Legislature position can be one of the easiest paths to the U.S. Congress and beyond, at least as long as the grueling nature of politics doesn't get to you first.

A Concluding Hope

At this point, I wish you the best of luck. I hope that you have at least a basic understanding of how the United States Government works, and hopefully you have cooked up a couple plans to build up our government where we consistently fall short. The world needs more good people in politics, people who are able to bring a fresh perspective, addressing old problems with new solutions, and help us strive more and more towards the ideals of democracy that the country was established on. It will be a difficult road to travel, don't get me wrong, but it is the difficulty that makes it worth doing. We all face huge challenges, and the future will hold so many more problems than we could even dream of today. It will also hold so many more solutions.

I wish you luck on your political journey, whether you simply wish to grow in your own knowledge or aspire to a higher office yourself. Just know that if you truly seek to better the nation and to create a system that is indeed as just and as fair and as good to as many citizens as it possibly can be, and if we all strive for that, we will eventually end up on the right track. The politics of today has become one of fear, one of divisiveness, and one of rapidly forming roadblocks, problems, and walls. While by no means do I expect, or would I even want, a country in which everyone agrees on everything, what I do hope for is a country where everyone can be on the same page, where everyone can argue from the same set of facts, and where everyone's personhood and identity can be valued even more so than their beliefs. I know that we might not agree on everything, and that's okay. In fact, that's great. But if we strive first and foremost to make the country a better one, one that works for everybody, no matter how we fight to do so, then we will once again find our country to be back on the right track. I wish you nothing but hope, prosperity, and peace, and I hope against hope that I can one day see you on the other side, in a better world.

Acknowledgements

A first book attempt is no easy feat, but I owe so many thanks to so many people who made the process significantly easier. Whether you knew it or not, you played a large role in the creation and inspiration of this text, keeping me on track and on task. In no particular order, I give thanks:

To my mom, Debbie. Your advice and edits helped to anchor my writing in reality, and our discussions always show me a better way of looking at the world.

To my dad, Robb. You're the first person to ever finish this book. Your dedication and belief in me has taken me far, always grounded in my first job: making people smile.

To my sister, Erin. You're a fantastic editor in your own right, both on the page and in video, which is really something considering you're good at so many other things. Keep following the ones that bring you joy.

To my partner, Ilana. Your belief in me is truly unwavering, and each and every day you remind me of what really matters. The process of writing this book has been great, but the time I get to spend with you is everything.

To my friend, Ethan. You know how to draw the activist out of the writer, and you remind me of the stakes of such an undertaking. Truly every word counts.

To my one-time professor, Dr. Pohler. I came to you with a bunch of words on a screen, and you pointed me the way towards making it into a book. Your knowledge has been invaluable as I've worked towards making this a reality.

To my editor, Alexis Rigoni. Dr. Pohler was right, you do truly have an eagle eye. You've saved me from death by a thousand punctuation-based wounds, and for that I'm truly grateful.

I'd also like to give a huge thank you to the people who have actually taught me politics in a classroom setting. I hope I haven't accidentally ripped off too much of your lectures, but know that if I have, it's meant as a compliment.

Finally, I'd like to give special thanks to everyone else in my life who has graciously reached out for productive political conversation throughout the years. Our conversations have informed my worldview more than you know. Thanks especially to Adam, Jackson, Collin, Tommy, Patrick, Jimmy, Jake, Kate, Aly, and so many more. Your friendship and our conversations have made me the person I am today, and for that I will always be in your debt. Let's keep improving the world together.

References

1. https://www.britannica.com/science/game-theory/The-prisoners-dilemma
2. https://projects.fivethirtyeight.com/redistricting-2022-maps/texas/
3. https://www.britannica.com/topic/collective-action-problem-1917157
4. https://www.oldest.org/politics/constitutions
5. https://www.law.uchicago.edu/news/lifespan-written-constitutions#:~:text= By%20our%20estimate%2C%20national%20constitutions,years%20since%20 1789%20%5B1%5D.
6. https://www.idea.int/sites/default/files/publications/the-fundamentals-of-a-constitution.pdf
7. https://www.archives.gov/founding-docs/constitution-transcript
8. https://www.propublica.org/article/clarence-thomas-scotus-undisclosed-lux ury-travel-gifts-crow
9. https://www.healthline.com/health/anxiety/effects-on-body#Immune-syste m
10. https://billofrightsinstitute.org/would-you-have-been-a-federalist-or-an-anti-federalist
11. https://ballotpedia.org/Home_rule
12. https://www.wanderlustworker.com/48-famous-failures-who-will-inspire-yo u-to-achieve/#:~:text=1%20%E2%80%94%20Abraham%20Lincoln&text=Bu t%20Lincoln%20didn't%20start,old%2C%20Lincoln%20lost%20his%20job.
13. https://www.senate.gov/legislative/MeasuresProposedToAmendTheConstit ution.htm
14. https://www.mountvernon.org/library/digitalhistory/quotes/topic/governm ent
15. https://www.newsweek.com/less-20-percent-americans-mostly-agree-either-major-political-party-poll-finds-1649568
16. https://nebraskalegislature.gov/about/history_unicameral.php
17. https://ballotpedia.org/Primary_election_types_by_state
18. https://members.parliament.uk/parties/Commons
19. https://www.cookpolitical.com/2020-national-popular-vote-tracker
20. https://www.nytimes.com/article/israel-government-elections.html?
21. https://www.e-ir.info/2018/05/25/one-party-state-is-it-good-or-bad-for-gov ernance/

22. https://education.nationalgeographic.org/resource/democracy-ancient-greece

23. https://www.opensecrets.org/elections-overview/reelection-rates

24. https://news.gallup.com/poll/1600/congress-public.aspx

25. https://www.ncsl.org/research/elections-and-campaigns/primary-types.aspx

26. https://ballotpedia.org/Top-four_primary

27. https://www.fairvote.org/third_party_and_independent_representation

28. https://ballotpedia.org/Timeline_of_announcements_in_the_presidential_election,_2020

29. https://www.nytimes.com/interactive/2019/08/02/us/politics/2020-democratic-fundraising.html

30. https://www.nytimes.com/2019/08/03/us/politics/democratic-candidates-fundraising.html

31. https://www.nytimes.com/2020/10/20/opinion/polarization-politics-americans.html

32. https://www.monmouth.edu/polling-institute/reports/monmouthpoll_nv_061219/

33. https://www.politico.com/story/2015/07/poll-gop-2016-name-recognition-donald-trump-jeb-bush-120573

34. https://www.icpsr.umich.edu/web/pages/instructors/setups2008/nominating.html

35. https://ballotpedia.org/State-by-state_redistricting_procedures

36. https://www.kansas-demographics.com/cities_by_population

37. https://upload.wikimedia.org/wikipedia/commons/thumb/5/51/How_To_Steal_An_Election.jpg/640px-How_To_Steal_An_Election.jpg

38. https://upload.wikimedia.org/wikipedia/commons/thumb/e/e1/Kansas_Congressional_Districts%2C_118th_Congress.tif/lossless-page1-640px-Kansas_Congressional_Districts%2C_118th_Congress.tif.png

39.

40. https://ballotpedia.org/Davis_v._Bandemer

41. https://ballotpedia.org/State-by-state_redistricting_procedures

42. oc.gov/classroom-materials/united-states-history-primary-source-timeline/new-nation-1783-1815/policies-and-problems-of-the-confederation-government/#:~:text=Congress%20claimed%20the%20following%20powers,settle%20disputes%20among%20the%20states.

43. https://www.history.com/topics/early-us/shays-rebellion

44. https://www.mountvernon.org/library/digitalhistory/digital-encyclopedia/article/shays-rebellion/#:~:text=A%20violent%20insurrection%20in%20the,states%20experienced%20similar%20economic%20hardships.

45. https://constitutioncenter.org/interactive-constitution/blog/the-day-the-constitution-was-ratified

46. https://www.americanbar.org/groups/public_education/resources/teacher_portal/educational_resources/executive_orders/

47. https://www.statutesandstories.com/blog_html/george-washingtons-first-executive-order/

48. https://potus-geeks.livejournal.com/1300800.html

49. https://www.presidency.ucsb.edu/statistics/data/executive-orders

50. https://millercenter.org/president/roosevelt/foreign-affairs

51. https://www.whitehouse.gov/about-the-white-house/presidents/theodore-ro osevelt/

52. https://www.whitehouse.gov/about-the-white-house/presidents/franklin-d-r oosevelt/

53. https://stars.library.ucf.edu/etd/4930/

54. https://www.encyclopedia.com/law/encyclopedias-almanacs-transcripts-and-maps/executive-branch#:~:text=Today%2C%20the%20executive%20branch%20consists,the%20government%2C%20such%20as%20the

55. https://web.archive.org/web/20201116050745/https://www.nbcnews.com/politics/congress/lawmakers-both-parties-want-postal-service-undo-changes-are-slowing-n1236086

56. https://slate.com/news-and-politics/2021/02/biden-cannot-fire-usps-louis-d ejoy.html

57. https://www.politico.com/news/2020/11/04/1-in-3-americans-lives-where-r ecreational-marijuana-legal-434004

58. https://www.drugpolicyfacts.org/chapter/crime_arrests#overlay=table/total_ arrests

59. https://www.google.com/search?q=i%27m+just+a+bill+lyrics&rlz=1C5CH FA_enUS810US810&ei=LKbyYvy4MqOpptQPlImvuAU&oq=i%27m+jus t+a+bill+ly&gs_lcp=Cgdnd3Mtd2l6EAEYADIFCAAQgAQyBQgAEIAE MgYIABAeEBYyBggAEB4QFjIGCAAQHhAWOgcIABBHELADOgcIAB CwAxBDOgoIABDkAhCwAxgBOg8ILhDUAhDIAxCwAxBDGAI6DAg uEMgDELADEEMYAjoICC4QgAQQ1AI6BQguEIAEOgQIABBDOgUI ABCGA0oECEEYAEoECEYYAVChAlj1C2CbEmgBcAB4AIABBb4gBtAK SAQMxLjKYAQCgAQHIARPAAQHaAQYIARABGAnaAQYIAhABGA g&sclient=gws-wiz

60. https://www.pewresearch.org/politics/2015/11/23/8-perceptions-of-the-pu blics-voice-in-government-and-politics/

61. https://peo.gov.au/understand-our-parliament/your-questions-on-notice/qu estions/can-someone-please-explain-the-four-models-of-representation-deleg ate-partisan-trustee-and-mirror-thank-you

62. https://www.house.gov/the-house-explained/the-legislative-process

63. https://www.senate.gov/reference/Index/Filibuster.htm#:~:text=The%20ter m%20filibuster%2C%20from%20a,prevent%20action%20on%20a%20bill.

64. https://www.senate.gov/about/powers-procedures/filibusters-cloture/overvie w.htm

65. https://www.thoughtco.com/longest-filibusters-in-us-history-3322332

66. https://www.senate.gov/artandhistory/history/minute/Great_Compromise. htm#:~:text=Their%20so%2Dcalled%20Great%20Compromise,in%20propo rtion%20to%20its%20population.

67. https://www.presidency.ucsb.edu/statistics/data/seats-congress-gainedlost-th e-presidents-party-mid-term-elections

68. https://crsreports.congress.gov/product/pdf/R/R46705#:~:text=Truman%2 0Scholars.22-,Congressional%20Service,years%20(1.8%20Senate%20terms).

69. https://guides.loc.gov/116th-congress-book-list#:~:text=The%20average%20 age%20of%20Members,a%20majority%20in%20the%20Senate.

70. https://www.census.gov/library/stories/2019/06/median-age-does-not-tell-t
he-whole-story.html#:~:text=The%20nation's%20median%20age%20was,is%
20more%20than%20a%20number.

71. https://history.house.gov/Institution/Presidents-Coinciding/Presidents-Coi
nciding/

72. https://www.annenbergclassroom.org/22nd-amendment/#:~:text=Passed%2
0by%20Congress%20in%201947,a%20total%20of%20eight%20years.

73. https://www.supremecourt.gov/about/buildinghistory.aspx

74. https://constitutioncenter.org/blog/why-does-the-supreme-court-have-nine-j
ustices

75. https://www.history.com/news/has-a-u-s-supreme-court-justice-ever-been-i
mpeached

76. https://news.gallup.com/poll/354908/approval-supreme-court-down-new-l
ow.aspx

77. https://news.gallup.com/poll/394103/confidence-supreme-court-sinks-histo
ric-low.aspx

78. https://ap.gilderlehrman.org/essay/andrew-jackson-and-constitution#:~:text
=They%20didn't%20attempt%20impeachment,state%20laws%20to%20Cher
okee%20lands.

79. https://www.history.com/news/7-things-you-may-not-know-about-the-trail-
of-tears#:~:text=Check%20out%20seven%20facts%20about%20this%20infa
mous%20chapter%20in%20American%20history.&text=Cherokee%20India
ns%20are%20forced%20from%20their%20homelands%20during%20the%20
1830's.

80. https://upload.wikimedia.org/wikipedia/commons/thumb/9/9c/Graph_of
_Bailey_Scores_of_Supreme_Court_Justices_1950-2011.png/640px-Graph
_of_Bailey_Scores_of_Supreme_Court_Justices_1950-2011.png

81. https://www.politico.com/f/?id=00000180-8d22-d337-a9cc-bfaa481a0000
&nname=playbook&nid=0000014f-1646-d88f-a1cf-5f46b7bd0000&nrid=0
000014e-f115-dd93-ad7f-f91513e50001&nlid=630318

82. https://www.nbcnews.com/politics/2020-election/inside-pete-buttigieg-s-pl
an-overhaul-supreme-court-n1012491

83. https://www.forbes.com/sites/alisondurkee/2022/03/15/most-americans-do
nt-think-supreme-court-acts-in-a-serious-and-constitutional-manner-and-wa
nt-reforms-poll-finds/?sh=4707eba35a8b

84. https://www.history.com/news/why-is-a-marathon-26-2-miles#:~:text=The
%20idea%20for%20the%20modern,After%20making%20his%20announcem
ent%2C%20the

85. https://www.historic-uk.com/CultureUK/The-Town-Crier/

86. https://www.worldhistory.org/Feudalism/

87. https://www.freedomforuminstitute.org/wp-content/uploads/2016/10/Th
e-First-Amendment-in-the-Colonial-press.pdf

88. https://www.spj.org/ethicscode.asp

89. https://www.businessinsider.com/animation-rise-partisanship-congress-hous
e-representatives-60-years-2016-4

90. https://www.history.com/this-day-in-history/cnn-launches

91. https://www.britannica.com/topic/CNN

92. https://www.britannica.com/topic/MSNBC

93. https://www.britannica.com/topic/Fox-News-Channel
94. https://www.poynter.org/fact-checking/media-literacy/2021/should-you-tru st-media-bias-charts/
95. https://www.statista.com/statistics/373814/cable-news-network-viewership-usa/
96. https://www.pewresearch.org/fact-tank/2021/01/12/more-than-eight-in-ten -americans-get-news-from-digital-devices/
97. https://www.ncbi.nlm.nih.gov/pmc/articles/PMC4183915/
98. https://www.statista.com/statistics/657111/fake-news-sharing-online/
99. https://news.mit.edu/2018/study-twitter-false-news-travels-faster-true-storie s-0308
100. https://constitution.congress.gov/constitution/amendment-1/
101. https://help.twitter.com/en/rules-and-policies/twitter-rules
102. https://transparency.fb.com/policies/community-standards/misinformation /
103. https://help.twitter.com/en/resources/addressing-misleading-info
104. https://medialiteracynow.org/2021-us-media-literacy-policy-report-shows-sig nificant-progress/
105. https://newseumed.org/medialiteracy
106. https://www.pbs.org/newshour/classroom/2021/02/lesson-plan-media-liter acy-news-thats-nice-to-know-news-you-need-to-know/
107. https://www.opensecrets.org/resources/learn/timeline
108. https://www.britannica.com/topic/political-machine
109. https://billofrightsinstitute.org/essays/william-boss-tweed-and-political-mac hines
110. https://www.americanheritage.com/political-machine-i-rise-and-fall-age-boss es
111. https://www.fec.gov/legal-resources/court-cases/buckley-v-valeo/
112. https://www.congress.gov/bill/107th-congress/house-bill/2356
113. https://www.fec.gov/legal-resources/court-cases/citizens-united-v-fec/#:~:tex t=The%20Court%20ultimately%20held%20in,or%20the%20appearance%20 of%20corruption.%22
114. https://www.fec.gov/legal-resources/court-cases/mccutcheon-et-al-v-fec/#:~: text=On%20April%202%2C%202014%2C%20the,and%20political%20actio n%20committees%20combined.
115. https://www.fec.gov/legal-resources/court-cases/speechnoworg-v-fec/#:~:tex t=Appellate%20court%20decision,to%20individuals'%20contributions%20t o%20SpeechNow.
116. https://www.opensecrets.org/political-action-committees-pacs/super-pacs/2 022
117. https://www.opensecrets.org/elections-overview/winning-vs-spending
118. https://www.statista.com/chart/22967/overall-election-spending-by-cycle-an d-party-affiliation/
119. https://www.churchlawcenter.com/nonprofit/differences-between-a-pac-and -a-501c4-social-welfare-organization/
120. https://thesciencesurvey.com/editorial/2022/02/01/its-time-to-ban-dark-mo ney-contributions/

121. https://www.majorityleader.gov/content/ten-years-after-citizens-united-hous e-democrats-call-senate-take-house-passed-government#:~:text=In%20Citize ns%20United%20v.,dark%20money%20to
122. https://www.insider.com/dog-mayors-of-america-2019-7
123. http://www.campaigninabox.us/blog/2018/1/28/what-does-it-cost-to-run-f or-city-council-and-win